101 GREAT CHOICES

WASHINGTON, D.C.

Jan Aaron

Printed on recyclable paper

PASSPORT BOOKS
a division of *NTC Publishing Group*
Lincolnwood, Illinois USA

Library of Congress Cataloging-in-Publication Data

Aaron, Jan.
    101 great choices : Washington, D.C. / Jan Aaron.
        p.   cm.
    Includes index.
    ISBN 0-8442-8992-2
    1. Washington (D.C.)--Guidebooks.   I. Title.
    F192. 3. A27 1995
    917.5304'4--dc20

                                            95-21792
                                            CIP

Cover & interior design by Nick Panos
Cover & interior illustration by Chris Horrie
Special thanks to Jan Farrington and Karen Ingebretsen
Maps: © 1995 MAGELLAN Geographix^{SM} Santa Barbara, CA

5 6 7 8 9 0 ML 9 8 7 6 5 4 3 2 1

Washington, D.C.: A Great Choice

You're walking down the Mall early one April morning, the marble monuments reflecting the glow of the sunrise. A shower of cherry blossoms falls across your path; a figure in a red jacket kneels beside the Vietnam Veterans Memorial tracing the etched names with his fingers; a jogger passes by with a large entourage. You have just seen the president. Later in the day, you might take a walk through his house. (Try doing that in Paris or London!)

You pass a grand dame of a hotel as a limousine drops off a well-tailored man or woman hurrying inside with a briefcase, late for a power breakfast. Your walk takes you past Depression-era government buildings, cafés beginning to open, sweatshirt vendors setting up their stalls, a group of Japanese students lining up to board a tourist bus. Turning the corner, you walk in lush woods; turn another corner, there are cobblestone streets and rowhouses with neat gardens; walk further and you're in front of a wonderful museum. Like many other museums, this one is free. Night falls and Washington shows its sparklier side, as music spills out of dance clubs and bars and same-sex couples holding hands stroll past tourists and businesspeople in buttoned-down suits.

Intercut images like these make Washington, D.C. a Great Choice. D.C. life continually interweaves sights that make the visitor at once familiar with the surroundings and also curious. The city has an edge and vitality like many others, but underneath it all the power and push of government make it a major attraction. At the same time, under this tough exterior beats the heart of a Southern belle to soften the edges and slow the pace. You'll taste the Southern side often these days in a number of restaurants that are reinventing Southern cuisine. The seemingly disparate aspects of politics and Southern gentility also make this ten-miles-square, diamond-shaped, garden-studded city a Great Choice. (There's a sadder side to all this Southernness, however; years after the advent of integration, D.C. really isn't.)

Washington, D.C. has practical aspects that make it even more of a great choice for tourists of all interests and income groups and ages. A substantial number of museums and other attractions are free; there are smart restaurants and cafés for all pocketbooks and a wealth of places to stay for a head of state or commoner; there is something for every shopper from the budget-minded to the big spender, from cutting-edge boutiques to places strictly for antiquities (no reference intended to our politicians). There's even a world of things to do with kids that adults like, too. *101 Great Choices* includes all this and more.

Of course, Washington, D.C. has its obvious great choices—for example, think of the Lincoln Memorial. It has been photographed, filmed, and described so often that you feel even on a first visit that it's an old friend. It and the other major monuments get only passing mention in this book, because another reason why D.C. is a Great Choice is that it has an offbeat side that goes beyond these standard sights. The bias of this book lies in that direction, and in helping you see the old familiar sights in a new way. Some of the Great Choices in this book are combined to make up a "Great Day." When it comes to Great Choices, it's hard to keep count in Washington, D.C.

But what really makes Washington, D.C. a Great Choice? It's the simple pleasure of walking around and enjoying the sights in this city, which grew from a simple sketch on a linen cloth to become the capital of a major world power. Have fun!

—Jan Aaron

The City at a Glance

Transportation

Getting to Washington, D.C.   Washington, D.C. is served by three airports—Washington National, Washington Dulles International, and Baltimore-Washington International (BWI). For most tourists, Washington National is the most convenient.

National is served by American West, American, Continental, Delta, Midwest Express, Northwest, TWA, United, and USAir Shuttle.

Most major carriers serve Dulles, including Aeroflot, British Airways, Air-France, Swissair, United, and USAir.

Airlines flying into BWI include Air Jamaica, Continental, Delta, Icelandair, Northwest, and TWA.

The cheapest way to get to the city from National is by Metro (short for Metrorail, the city's rapid rail system). You can walk to the Metro station or take the free airport shuttle that services each terminal. It generally costs $1 to $1.50, depending on time of day.

Metrobus, the city's bus system, also serves the airport; the bus stop is in front of the main terminal. For 24-hour Metrobus information, call (703) 685-8000; for shuttlebus and parking information, call (703) 271-4300.

No public transportation operates from Dulles, but both National and Dulles are served at all times by Washington Flyer buses; the twenty-minute ride from National to downtown costs $8 ($14 round trip); from Dulles, the thirty-minute rides costs $16 ($26 round trip). MasterCard and Visa are accepted. For information, call (703) 685-1400.

From BWI, Airport Connection buses leave every ninety minutes for 1517 K St. NW; the sixty-five-minute ride costs $14 ($25 round trip). Traveler's checks and cash are accepted. For information, call (301) 441-2345.

Free shuttle service is provided between the airport terminals and the train station at BWI. Trains run between BWI and Union Station in Washington, D.C. from 6 a.m. to 11 p.m. The cost of this ride is $9 on Amtrak and $4.25 on MARC (Maryland Rail Commuter Service). For Amtrak information, call (800) USA-RAIL; for MARC information, call (800) 325-RAIL.

Some hotels have complimentary limousine service to and from airports; check when you make reservations.

Taxis are available at all three airports. Cab fare downtown from National costs approximately $8; from Dulles, $45; from BWI, $50.

Many seasoned travelers believe that train travel is the most pleasant way to travel. More than fifty trains a day pull into the restored Union Station on Capitol Hill (50 Massachusetts Ave. NE). For first-class and club service passengers traveling to and from New York, Washington, D.C., Chicago, and Philadelphia, Amtrak offers sleek Metrolounges with the art deco decor of fabled trains of the past and modern conveniences such as telephones, a conference room, and an online computer network.

Amtrak trains connect Washington, D.C. to most other parts of the country via Union Station. In many locations, you may choose either regular or Metroliner (faster) train service.

Amtrak offers a number of special fares throughout the year, so be sure to inquire when you call about tickets. For information, call (202) 484-7540 or (800) USA-RAIL.

Washington, D.C. is an important terminal for Greyhound Bus Lines (1005 1st St. NE); check with your local Greyhound depots in suburban Silver Spring and Laurel, Maryland and Springfield, Virginia. For Greyhound information in Washington, D.C., call (301) 565-2662.

Getting around Washington, D.C. Pierre Charles L'Enfant, the French engineer who designed the city, laid it out in a gridlike pattern, divided into four quadrants (Northwest, Northeast, Southwest, Southeast—abbreviated NW, NE, SW, SE). The lettered streets run east to west; the numbered streets, north to south. Avenues named for U.S. states run diagonally, and intersect with the east-west and north-south streets at graceful traffic circles located throughout the city. This seems to confuse some visitors, so here's something to guide you. Geographically, the U.S. Capitol building is the center of Washington, D.C.'s streets. North and South Capitol streets divide the city into east and west, and the Mall and East Capitol Street sever it north and south.

Washington, D.C. is a wonderful city for walking. You'll want to explore the Dupont Circle-Kalorama area, with its side streets full of former millionaires' mansions, some of which are now intriguing museums. You can stroll Georgetown's lanes and meander the towpath beside the C&O Canal. There's much fun in rambling around Adams-Morgan, where tree-shaded streets are lined with quaint rowhouses and small cafés serving ethnic foods are interspersed with shops featuring antiques. Downtown's hectic side has its antidote in wonderful, walkable parks. Or, you can get away from it all on the magnificent wooded trails in Rock Creek Park, which weave a ribbon of green through the city.

Most attractions in every neighborhood are accessible by Metrorail (Metro), D.C.'s cheap, clean, and efficient subway system. Metro also connects the city with the nearby Maryland and Virginia suburbs. Metro stations are marked with a bold M on a tall pillar. To use the Metro, you must purchase a farecard from a vending machine; maps and charts explaining how to use the machines are in every station. (There's usually a Metro attendant around to ask, too, if you need help.) Fares start at $1 and go up according to destination; if you plan to use the Metro a lot, buy one of the multiple-fare cards. To use a farecard, dip it into the slot on the turnstile upon entering and leaving the station; an electronic reader calculates the distance and fare. Be sure not to misplace your card before you exit—you will need it to get out. (If you do lose it, you will have to pay the maximum applicable fare.) Trains operate every ten minutes, from 5:30 a.m. to midnight Monday through Friday and 8 a.m. to midnight Saturday and Sunday. (If you are traveling late in the evening, ask an attendant what time the last train leaves the station from which you'll be departing.)

Metrobus's routes and schedules are timed to coincide with Metrorail's for coordinated service. You can pick up Metrobus and Metrorail route maps at the stations and at a number of sightseeing attractions. For bus and subway information, call (202) 637-5700.

Taxis in Washington, D.C. operate on the zone system, and by law, zone maps and rates must be posted in cabs. (There's a $1 surcharge for each additional passenger and a $1.25 surcharge during evening rush hours, 3:30 to 6:30 p.m.) But unless you know the city, how do you know when one zone ends and the next begins? Here's some advice: When you get in a taxi, ask how many zones your ride will cover. Usually, the drivers are honest. However, if at the end of your journey you think you have been overcharged, ask for an official receipt with the company's and driver's names and the business telephone number. Then call the D.C. Taxi Commission with your complaint (202) 767-8319.

For free tourist information, write or call the Washington Convention and Visitors Association, 1212 New York Ave. NW, Suite 600, Washington, D.C. 20005-3992; (202) 789-7000. In Washington, D.C., get information at the new White House Visitors Center at the Department of Commerce, 1450 Pennsylvania Ave. NW. For information, call (202) 208-1631 or (202) 208-1633. In addition, many hotels and sightseeing attractions stock a selection of pamphlets and maps.

Neighborhoods

Stationed above the city, the eye of a camera sweeping Washington, D.C. would see masses of tourists making their way along a park- and pool-lined grassy strip called the Mall. The camera would catch a few braver visitors drifting off into the surrounding neighborhoods to experience the rich diversity and history that give this city unique charm. Be among the brave. Stray from the herd. If you don't, you won't experience the real Washington, D.C.

The Mall   The Mall is not a neighborhood, but a strip of parklike land between Constitution and Independence avenues, stretching two and a half miles from the Capitol to the Lincoln Memorial. The Mall plays a central role in the lives of not only tourists but Washingtonians as well. Great museums border the Mall and great monuments are located on it.

Capitol Hill/Northeast   This huge triangular area is formed by North Capitol Street, East Capitol Street, and the D.C.-Maryland border. Here are the Capitol, Supreme Court, Library of Congress, and Senate and House office buildings; amusing cafés, and bars, lovely old row-houses and parks, as well as Eastern Market and the restored Union Station. Take time for splendor in the grass at the U.S. National Arboretum in the east; see the unusual Walter Reed Medical Museum in the Northeast area of Shepherd's Park.

Anacostia/Southeast   This neighborhood extends from the Anacostia River to Pennsylvania Avenue on the north and Southern Avenue on the southeast. Named for early Native American inhabitants, the area dates back to John Smith's arrival in 1607. Here are the Frederick Douglass National Historic Site and the Smithsonian's Anacostia Museum. The neighborhood has problems and is best explored in daylight with a couple of friends.

Southwest/The Mall   This neighborhood south of the Mall includes the award-winning Arena Stage theater, as well as Banneker Circle and L'Enfant Plaza, a "work of park" in progress, and the delightful Victorian U.S. Botanic Gardens. To the west is the waterfront, with boats, seafood markets, and restaurants.

Foggy Bottom/West End   Between Pennsylvania and Virginia avenues, from 18th to 25th streets NW: This is where you'll find the Kennedy Center, Watergate Hotel and elegant Watergate shopping arcade, George Washington University, and Corcoran Gallery. Here, too, are the State Department building, Federal Reserve, and National Academy of Sciences. The northern part of this neighborhood nudges into Georgetown.

Downtown   Located between 4th Street and 17th Street NW and from Constitution Avenue north to M Street, this neighborhood has been substantially revitalized in the last few years. By day, it's a buttoned-down business district; by night, it swings with new clubs and restaurants. You'll want to investigate the FBI, National Archives, and White House, and shop for trinkets at the Old Post Office Pavilion.

Chinatown   You can't miss the bright seventy-five-foot-wide Friendship Arch, which straddles H Street at 7th Street and looms over tiny eight-block-long Chinatown, bordered by G, E, F, and 8th streets NW. The restaurants' decor won't win any awards, but the food might. Interesting shops sell Chinese goods. (Note that Chinese New Year is celebrated in late January or February.)

Dupont Circle   In the 1800s, millionaires gravitated here and left their mansions behind as souvenirs. In the blocks radiating off the circle and along Connecticut Avenue, from N through T streets NW, the mélange includes heterosexuals and homosexuals, antiques, books, music stores, restaurants, galleries, and museums, including the Phillips Collection.

Embassy Row   Most of the city's 153 foreign embassies are located in former mansions along Massachusetts Avenue NW, west of Dupont Circle, between Sheridan Circle and Observatory Circle. Embassy Row is a neighborhood made for walking and for photographing the façades of diplomats' digs.

Adams-Morgan   Located between 16th Street and Connecticut Avenue east of Kalorama Park, Adams-Morgan, is the outpost Washingtonians like to compare to Greenwich Village. It's more of an ethnic melting pot than other D.C. neighborhoods, as seen in its funky mix of restaurants, boutiques, and a laid-back hip atmosphere.

Georgetown   Georgetown, in the extreme west of D.C., bounded by the Potomac River on the south and Rock Creek Park on the east, had its first heyday as a prosperous seaport predating the city of Washington, D.C. It became fashionable again after World War II. Now it's a headquarters for hot nightlife, smart shops, trendy restaurants, and tiny old homes that fetch huge prices. Visit neoclassical Tudor Place, once home to a granddaughter of Martha Washington, and stop at Dumbarton Oaks to smell the roses—a thousand of them. Tour the Old Stone House; cruise the C&O Canal.

Upper Northwest   This neighborhood extends from north of Georgetown to Chevy Chase and the Maryland border. The gracious residential area running north along Connecticut Avenue from Calvert Street NW is Woodley Park. Visit the panda exhibit at the National Zoological Park; tour the Washington National Cathedral; and explore Hillwood, a trove of Russian treasures. At the northern end of this neighborhood is Friendship Heights.

Shaw   This northwest low-income neighborhood is bounded by North Capitol Street on the east, 15th Street on the west, and M Street on the south. This area was the center of the African-American business and retail life until the end of segregation in the 1950s. Badly scarred by the riots following the assassination of Martin Luther King, Jr., Shaw has hit the comeback trail since the new Frank Reeves Municipal Building opened in 1986. Small experimental theater companies, cafés, boutiques, and craft shops find homes here, as does the stunning Community Church. Don't roam alone at night.

Le Droit Park   Le Droit Park is located north of Florida Avenue to W Street between 2nd and 5th streets NW. This neighborhood is listed in the National Register of Historic Places. To the north is Howard University.

Virginia & Maryland   Much of our nation's early history has its origins in Virginia so you'll want to explore your roots at the sites across the border. Maryland's claims to fame exceed its famous crab cakes and suburban status for Washingtonians—it's great for antiques. Both are easy excursions from D.C., adding to their appeal.

Weather

The two top seasons for visiting D.C. are spring and fall. Winters have more rain than snow, but they are also unpredictable and there can be blizzards. The good news is that hotel rates also dip when the temperature does. Temperate weather begins in April and extends through October. Spring is famous for its cherry blossom hoopla; it's also very crowded and expensive. In the summer, there's high humidity. (Washington, D.C. must be why air conditioning was invented.) Fall is absolutely lovely, with warm days, cool nights, and blazing foliage. For a D.C.-area weather report, call (202) 936-1212.

Here are D.C.'s average high temperatures in degrees Fahrenheit:

January—43°	July—87°
February—44°	August—84°
March—53°	September—78°
April—64°	October—68°
May—75°	November—55°
June—83°	December—45°

Washington, D.C. tourist attire is basically informal. However, many restaurants require men to wear a jacket and tie. Nightclubs, restaurants, and theaters range from rather dressy to casual. For sightseeing and informal dining, you can wear neat shorts or jeans. Where there's a dress code for an establishment, it's included in the write-up that appears in this book.

For summer sun protection, take a hat and sunscreen. In winter, dress in layers, easy to adapt to indoor-outdoor temperatures; bring warm, rainproof outerwear, a muffler, gloves, a hat, and waterproof boots. For every season, you'll need comfortable walking shoes. Year-round, pack an umbrella, traveler's check company's refund number, medications you need, and prescriptions in case you run out. Take a photo I.D.; you may need it for some attractions.

Banking/Currency

Dulles International Airport has a currency exchange for changing your money into United States currency upon arrival; however, foreign exchange bureaus, common in Europe, are not easily found in the United States. In the D.C. area, places to exchange currency include Thomas Cook, (1800 T St. NW;

Monday-Friday, 9 a.m.-5 p.m.) and Union Station opposite Gate G; Monday-Friday 9 a.m.-5 p.m.; Sunday noon-6 p.m.

It's always best and safest to carry your cash in traveler's checks. Many places in D.C. (and elsewhere) won't take personal checks.

American Express card holders can cash personal checks at any full-service American Express office. In Washington, D.C., you'll find these offices at 1150 Connecticut Ave. NW (202) 457-1300; 5300 Wisconsin Ave. NW (202) 362-4000; and 1776 Pennsylvania Ave. NW (202) 289-8800. Short of funds? American Express MoneyGrams allow travelers to send and receive money from more than seventy countries.

Major world banks, including Citibank and Bank of America, have branches in Washington, D.C. Banking hours are generally Monday-Friday, 9 a.m.-3 p.m., but some banks stay open until 6 p.m. on Fridays, and a few are open on Saturday mornings. All banks are closed on legal holidays. Most automated teller machines in D.C. accept Cirrus cards (800-4-CIRRUS) and/or Plus (800-THE-PLUS).

Sightseeing

Taking a narrated tour is a good way to survey the city. Whether you're seeking a special-interest tour, going out of D.C., or just want to take it easy, hop on a narrated tour.

Old Town Trolley Tours: Copies of old-fashioned trackless trolleys follow a fixed route around the Mall and beyond to such sights as Arlington National Cemetery and the Washington National Cathedral, making a total of sixteen stops. You may stay on and listen to the two-hour narration, or exit and reboard as often as you like within the loop and join a later trolley; they run every thirty minutes. From Memorial Day to Labor Day, the hours are 9 a.m.-5 p.m., Monday-Thursday, and 9 a.m.-5:30 p.m., Friday-Saturday. Fares are $16 for adults and $8 for children ages five-twelve; (301) 985-3020.

Tourmobile: This company has an agreement with the National Park Service to provide shuttle service to eighteen attractions between the Capitol and Arlington National Cemetery. Shuttles run between 9:30 a.m. and 4:30 p.m. Fares are $8.50 for adults and $4 for children three-eleven; (202) 554-7950.

Gray Line Sightseeing Tours: Gray Line conducts a similar on-and-off-again two-hour, fourteen-stop trolley tour that includes the major sights plus Arlington Cemetery and the National Zoological Park. The tours run seven days a week every thirty minutes, except in winter, when they are every hour. Fares are $16 for adults and $8 for children ages three-eleven; (202) 289-1995, (800) 862-1400.

Gray Line also operates four-hour daily tours year-round in comfortable motorcoaches. One tour focuses on Washington, D.C., Embassy Row, and Arlington National Cemetery; one tour focuses on Alexandria and Mount Vernon. Fares are $22 for adults and $12 for children. A nine-hour tour combines both. Fares for the nine-hour tour are $38 for adults and $20 for children; (202) 289-1995, (800) 862-1400.

Gray Line operates a number of special-interest tours, including the Black Heritage tour (see page 13), Washington After Dark tour, and multilingual tours. Gray Line also offers longer trips to Monticello and other historic sites beyond Washington, D.C.; (202) 289-1995, (800) 862-1400.

All About Town, Inc.: This company conducts tours similar to Gray Line's, in glass-topped coaches. All About Town is located at 519 Sixth St. NW; (202) 393-3696.

Capitol River Cruises: Boats depart from Washington Harbor for ninety-minute narrated tours offering a river view of famous landmarks. Tours operate daily, April 1-October 31, every hour, starting at noon on weekdays and 11 a.m. on Saturdays and Sundays. It's best to double-check the schedule. Fares are $8 for adults and $5 for children ages three-twelve; (301) 460-7447.

Dandy Cruises: Moored in Old Town Alexandria, Dandy Cruises offers sleek vessels that can cruise under D.C.'s bridges and sail up the Potomac to Georgetown. Cruises operate seven days a week, year-round. Prices start at about $32 for a weekday lunch cruise to about $69 for a Saturday night dinner-dance cruise; (703) 683-6090.

Spirit of Washington Cruises: Moored at Pier 4, 6th and Water streets SW in D.C.'s harbor, this company offers cruises on the Potomac. You can get a deckside view of the area's landmarks with your lunch or dinner. The evening cruises include live entertainment. Cruise prices range from around $28 for a weekday lunch to $54 for a weekend dinner. Cruises operate from March through December; (202) 554-8000.

The Black History Recreation Tour is not a tour in the usual sense of the word, but a listing of places that trace African-

American history in Washington, D.C. from the days of slavery to the New Deal. (One of the houses on this trail, the Frederick Douglass National Historic Site, is featured on page 19.) Brochures on the trail are available through the National Park Service, 1100 Ohio Dr. SW, Washington, D.C. 20242; (202) 619-7222.

The Construction Watch Tour and Site Seeing Tour are conducted by the National Building Museum during fair weather. On a Construction Watch tour, architects and project managers join the tour-goers to explain a variety of sites in different stages of construction. On a Site Seeing tour, architectural historians lead groups to visit famous buildings and neighborhoods. Tours take place once or twice a month. Prices range from about $7 to $60 per person for a bus tour with a box lunch. Reservations are a must. For information and a calendar of events, call (202) 272-2448, ext. 3304.

The Smithsonian Resident Associate Program offers a variety of walking and bus tours in and about Washington; (202) 357-3030.

The Guide Service of Washington, D.C., (202) 628-2842, will provide a guide to accompany you in your car, van, or bus. Prices range from $98 for a four-hour tour to $142 for an eight-hour tour.

Safety/Emergencies

Everyone knows Washington, D.C.'s reputation for crime, but this city can be safe and hospitable as well. If you use common sense you should have a successful, happy visit. The Washington, D.C. Convention and Visitor's Association offers these tips:

Become familiar with your surroundings; carefully study maps and guide books before starting out.

Do not display cash openly; use traveler's checks wherever possible.

Park in well-lit areas.

Remove all personal belongings from your car or lock them in the trunk.

Always lock your car and take your key.

At night, travel in well-lit areas and don't walk alone.

Aggressive panhandling is discouraged by D.C. laws. Please refrain from direct contact with panhandlers.

Secure valuables in a hotel safe or safety deposit box.

Locate the fire and emergency exits at your hotel, and study evacuation procedures.

If you detect any suspicious activity or noise at your hotel, contact the front desk or hotel security.

Obviously, take from this list what is helpful to you. You should always keep your wallet or handbag secure, carry only one credit card and a few traveler's checks at a time (leave the others at the hotel), and avoid wearing a lot of flashy jewelry.

Note: Washington is one of the most accessible cities in the world for disabled travelers. Most monuments and museums are accessible to the disabled. Metrorail has facilities for seeing-, hearing-, and mobility-impaired passengers. This includes elevator access from street entrances and between the platforms at multi-level stations.

EMERGENCY INFORMATION
Police   911
Fire Department   911
Ambulance   911
Metro Transit Police   (202) 962-2121
Medical Referral Service   (202) 362-8677
Dental Referral Service   (202) 547-7615
Drug/Alcohol Hotline   (202) 783-1300
Poison Control   (202) 625-3333
Traveler's Aid   (202) 546-3120
People's Drug   (202) 628-0720; (202) 785-1466
(24-hour pharmacies)

HOLIDAYS
New Year's Day   January 1
Martin Luther King's Birthday   third Monday in January
Lincoln's Birthday   February 12
Washington's Birthday   third Monday in February
Memorial Day   last Monday in May
Independence Day   July 4
Labor Day   first Monday in September
Columbus Day   second Monday in October
Election Day   first Tuesday in November
Veteran's Day   November 11
Thanksgiving Day   fourth Thursday in November
Christmas   December 25

How to Use This Book

101 Great Choices: Washington, D.C. is your guide to a sampling of the best that the city has to offer: accommodations, dining, parks & gardens, museums & galleries and other attractions.

Entries are arranged by neighborhoods, from Capitol Hill/Northeast moving to the southwest and wending upward as a tourist in D.C. might. Just pick a neighborhood or street and you will find something interesting to do, whether it's sightseeing, dining, snacking, shopping, hiking, or experiencing a special entertainment. Several entries send you to more than one neighborhood (for example, the entries on bookstore/cafés and budget tips) rather than a single location. They are listed in the neighborhood in which the adventure starts. Attractions are grouped into eleven categories, each identified by a small icon at the top of each entry.

If you want to go directly to the best places to eat, shop, take the kids, and so on, use the handy chart below, which list the attractions in this guide by **category** and choice **number.**

Accommodations
14, 36, 40, 47, 51, 56, 58, 67, 71, 91

Children
15, 30, 41, 42, 73, 94

Dining
5, 35, 37, 44, 48, 50, 52, 55, 59, 60, 63, 68, 69, 74, 75, 76, 87, 89

Entertainment & Nightlife
23, 27, 32, 38, 39, 80, 88

Miscellany
7, 8, 9, 16, 19, 29, 33, 43, 45, 62, 81, 92, 100

Museums & Galleries
4, 6, 13, 18, 21, 22, 24, 25, 31, 34, 46, 49, 57, 61, 64, 66, 95

Out of Town
97, 98, 99

Parks & Gardens
3, 28, 85, 90, 101

Shopping
65, 82, 84, 96

Sightseeing
1, 2, 10, 11, 12, 17, 20, 26, 53, 54, 70, 72, 77, 78, 79, 86, 93

Sports & Recreation
83

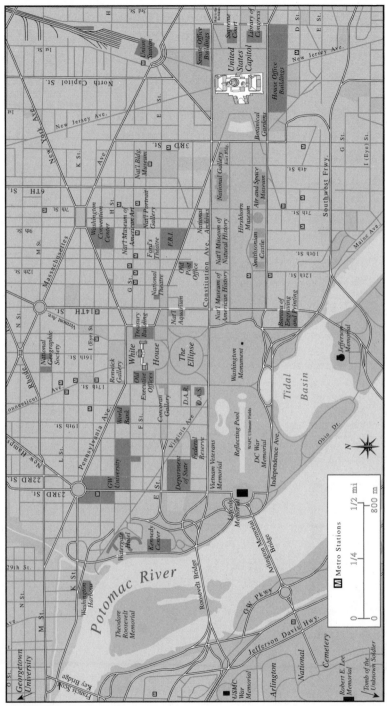

Washington, D.C.

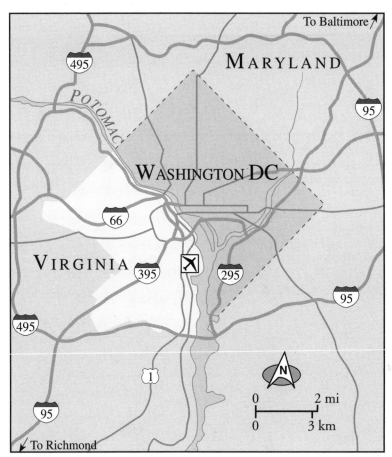

Washington, D.C. Vicinity

101
GREAT
CHOICES
WASHINGTON, D.C.

1 / Be a VIP

Capitol, White House, Bureau of Engraving and Printing, FBI, Kennedy Center

Make your first great choice before you leave home by getting VIP passes to some of D.C.'s most popular attractions: the Capitol, the White House, the Bureau of Engraving and Printing, the J. Edgar Hoover FBI Building, and the John F. Kennedy Center for the Performing Arts.

This is not insider's information; hundreds of people know about these tours and write for passes to them. So get your letter in the mail as much as six months before your visit—each senator and congressional representative gets only a limited number of tickets. Despite the competition, it's worth a shot. You may not get VIP passes, but you might get an invitation to drop by your representative's office. While there, you may be able to get passes that allow you to visit the Senate and House galleries while Congress is in session.

Send requests to your elected officials at the U.S. House of Representatives, Washington, D.C. 20515 and the U.S. Senate, Washington, D.C. 20510. Be sure to mention the exact dates you wish to visit and the number of people in your party. Also request gallery passes and literature on D.C. attractions. (Some senators' and representatives' offices handle these requests by telephone either locally or through their Washington offices.)

Here's what VIP tour-goers get:

The Capitol   The tour commences at 8 a.m. and lasts fifteen minutes longer than the regular tour. It includes both the House and Senate chambers; the regular tour visits only one.

The White House   VIP tours take place between 8:15-9a.m.; guided tours are more extensive than regular self-guided tours (see page 55).

The Bureau of Engraving and Printing, FBI, and Kennedy Center   VIP passes mean you are whisked in without waiting in very long lines. They can save you an hour or more.

2 / Off to a Great Start: Day 1, Part 1

The Mall

Put the Mall first on your list. It deserves this position. Yet, wouldn't it be great to get an almost-private viewing of this famous two-mile swath of bright green grass, reflecting pools, and wide gravel paths that connect the Capitol to the Washington, D.C. monuments? To see it all without the distraction of t-shirt hawkers and caravans of tourist buses?

A dawn walk allows you to experience the Mall the way few visitors do—when there's the relaxed feeling of a city just coming awake and the hustle of the tourism business is still hours away. Aside from the intimacy, this first walk helps you get your bearings and plan your visits to the fourteen museums in and around the Mall. Museums open at 10 a.m. (See the Mall in the evening, too, when the monuments are floodlit; the Lincoln Memorial is a special knockout at night.)

For your dawn visit, you can stroll to the West Mall and pay homage to the sparkling marble monuments honoring three famous presidents—Washington, Lincoln, and Jefferson. You also can pay a visit to "the Wall"—the striking Vietnam Veterans Memorial (see page 28). This memorial is open twenty-four hours a day.

Walk over to the beautiful Tidal Basin and watch the sunrise tint its rippling waters. Enjoy splendid views of the monuments you've just seen close-up and of the city further on. This is where you'll find Washington's greatest concentration of cherry trees, a gift from Japan. From mid-March to mid-April, the blossoms from six hundred breeze-tossed cherry trees cause petal blizzards here.

Now it's time for a wave at the White House; then head off to a special breakfast at a restaurant of your choice.

The Mall

The Mall runs east and west from the Capitol to Potomac Park and is bounded on the north and south by Constitution and Independence avenues.

3 / A Park for Greta Garbo
U.S. National Arboretum

Remember Greta Garbo's oft-quoted "I 'vant' to be alone?" If the retiring movie queen only had known about the U.S. National Arboretum. . . . Except for the masses of tourists in late April, when the azaleas and rhododendrons bloom, its vast expanse of woodland and gardens on the banks of the Anacostia River is nearly empty.

Established in 1927 as a research and educational center, the 444-acre arboretum is a shifting glow of color through the seasons. You'll find magnolias, crab apples, peonies, dogwoods, dwarf conifers, blazing leaves in fall, and, in a separate pavilion, the multi-million-dollar National Bonsai Collection.

Fifty-three of these meticulously manicured trees were a Bicentennial gift to the United States from the people of Japan. Some are more than three hundred years old.

The arboretum's delightful herb garden includes a historic rose garden with a contemporary knot garden modeled after a sixteenth-century English one.

Berry bushes lure birds to the National Bird Garden; trails lead past rare ferns to the acropolis, with twenty-two of the original U.S. Capitol columns designed by Benjamin Latrobe. (They were moved here because they were considered too fragile to remain in their original location.)

Other highlights include the New American Garden, the American Friendship Garden, and the 150-specimen Gotelli collection of dwarf conifers.

Capitol Hill/Northeast

U.S. National Arboretum, 3501 New York Ave. NE; (202) 475-4815. Open weekdays, 8 a.m.-5 p.m.; weekends and holidays, 10 a.m.-5 p.m.; bonsai collection, 10 a.m.-3:30 p.m. daily. Closed December 25. Free. Take buses B-2, B-4, B-5 from the Stadium-Armory station to Bladensburg Road and R Street; or take a taxi. Free parking; you can drive through arboretum; frequent tours; workshops, including bonsai classes; shop.

4 / At Home with Ken and Barbie (and Other Archival Greats)

Library of Congress

The president and first lady of Toyland, Ken and Barbie, live at 101 Independence Ave. SW, not far from the White House. As first dolls in their line, they are in the permanent exhibit at the Library of Congress. They are among the one hundred million items that make the library's collection the largest in the world.

Four hundred items are added every hour to the library's collection, which includes twenty-eight million books and pamphlets in 470 languages, fifteen hundred flutes, five Stradivarius violins, and the world's largest collection of comic books. Also among the holdings are letters of famous diplomats, films, photos, recordings, and other memorabilia. The library is open to researchers over eighteen. (Younger visitors are welcome at exhibits and tours.)

The collection, started as a single reference room for members of Congress, was funded in 1800 with $5,000. It was destroyed in 1814, when the British burned the city, then reincarnated when Thomas Jefferson donated his collection of 6,487 books as a replacement. The elaborate Italian Renaissance/Beaux Arts Thomas Jefferson Building, opened in 1897, holds the Main Reading Room, a hushed, marble-lined octagon with a graceful 160-foot-high dome. The John Adams Building, added in 1939, contains African, Asian, Far Eastern, and Hebraic collections. The James Madison Memorial Building, opened in 1980, houses extensive photography and film archives. The building's Mary Pickford Theater shows film classics free of charge. For film information, call (202) 707-5677. *Capitol Hill/Northeast*

Library of Congress, 1st Street and Independence Avenue SE; (202) 707-5000. Twenty-two-minute orientation film in Madison Bldg., Independence Avenue and between 1st and 2nd streets, runs every half-hour 9 a.m.-9:30 p.m. weekdays; Saturday 8:30 a.m.-5 p.m. Tours from Madison Building 10 a.m.-1 p.m. and 3 p.m. Shop and café in Madison Building. Metro Stations: Union Station or Capitol South.

5 / Be Bowled Over by Bean Soup

Eating in the Capitol and Nearby

Is this the best bean soup in the country? I doubt it. But is it the most famous? Absolutely.

Some people believe you can't say you've done Washington unless you've sipped a bowl of bean soup—not just any bean soup, but the bean soup that's "bean" on the Congressional menu since the early 1900s.

No one knows how the lowly bean soup became VIP soup; some credit its status to the culinary tastes and clout of a couple of senators (Minnesota's Knute Nelson and Idaho's Fred Thomas Dubois). Whatever the real story, bean soup is served daily by order of Congress in all the dining rooms and cafeterias in the Senate office buildings.

One place to sip bean soup is the vaulted-ceiling Refectory, first floor, Senate side of the Capitol; (202) 224-4870. Open 8 a.m.-4 p.m., later if the Senate is in session. You might even catch a glimpse of a politician in the halls. (Senators sip and sup in the Senate Dining Room.) Burgers, sandwiches and hot entrées, and pies are also served.

Here are other places in and about the Capitol to satisfy a bean soup craving or snack attack, or eat a full meal:

Dirksen Senate Office Building South Buffet Room, 1st and C streets NE; (202) 224-4249. Lunch Monday-Friday, 11:30 a.m.-2:30 p.m. Features a tasty all-you-can-eat buffet and bean soup.

House of Representatives Restaurant, Room 118, south end of the Capitol; (202) 225-6300. Monday-Friday, breakfast, lunch, and dinner when Congress is in session; Monday-Friday, 9 a.m.-2:30 p.m. when not in session. Elegant-looking decently priced restaurant; eclectic menu features ethnic and American fare: sandwiches, salads, and—you guessed it—bean soup.

Metro Station for all sites: Union Station or Capitol South.

Capitol Hill/Northeast

6 / Brush Up Your Shakespeare

Folger Shakespeare Library

Paul Philippe Cret's Greek-inspired art deco architecture at the Folger Shakespeare Library hides a surprise. Even with nine exterior bas-reliefs depicting scenes from Shakespeare's plays, and a statue of the funster Puck from *A Midsummer Night's Dream*, you'd never guess at the Elizabethan riches inside. The interiors magically conjure Shakespearean times with a three-story inn-yard theater and Elizabethan decor.

In 1930, Henry Clay Folger, a former Standard Oil chairman and Shakespearean enthusiast, and his wife, Emily, gave their collection to the American people.

The Folger Shakespeare Library contains the world's largest collection of the Bard's printed works. The initial Folger donation of 93,000 books, 50,000 prints and engravings, and thousands of manuscripts has grown to more than 260,000 relevant works.

In the Great Hall galleries, changing exhibits display selections from the collection. Look here for Sir Joshua Reynolds's portrait of great Shakespearean actor David Garrick.

Concerts, readings, and other Shakespearean-themed events take place periodically in the inn-yard theater. An open house in April marks the Bard's birthday.

The Shakespeare Theater that used to perform at the Folger moved to larger quarters in 1992. Under the direction of Michael Kahn, it offers three Shakespearean and one other classical work each year in top-notch productions with famous actors. In the summer, the company presents free Shakespeare in Rock Creek Park (see page 92).

Capitol Hill/Northeast

Folger Shakespeare Library, 201 East Capitol St. SE (between 2nd and 3rd streets); (202) 544-7077. Monday-Saturday 10 a.m.-4 p.m. Free. Shop. Metro Station: Capitol South.

Shakespeare Theater, 450 7th St. NW (between D and E streets); (202) 393-2700. Metro Station: Archives-Navy Memorial.

7 / Celebrate Saturday

Eastern Market

The big deal in Washington on Saturday morning is a crack-of-dawn visit to Eastern Market, not far from Capitol Hill. Farmers bring their fruits, vegetables, flowers, and homemade goodies to sell outdoors at this market. Inside the 1873 building there's a pricey meat and produce market and an art gallery. But there are other reasons to get up for Eastern Market.

The traditional Eastern Market ritual includes a delicious breakfast at the misleadingly named Market Lunch. Latecomers have a long wait in line—and with good reason. One taste of the state-of-the-art blueberry buckwheat pancakes is enough to go into raptures over. You get three or four pancakes piled high and topped with fresh fruit and whipped cream (about $3-$5). In mild weather, eat at an outdoor table while reading the *Washington Post* and checking out the scene.

Should you find yourself dozing off while in line, buy a cup of coffee at the nearby pass-through window. (*Line-haters alert:* Not far from Eastern Market is a pleasant café, Bread and Chocolate. No waiting. Sit inside or outside for delicious French-Swiss inspired dishes and frothy cappuccino in a bowl-size cup.)

You also can enjoy live jazz and shop for arts and crafts and antiques at Eastern Market on Saturdays. On Sundays, food vendors are replaced by a flea market featuring quite an assortment of secondhand stuff.

Everything is less hectic during the week, and Market Lunch is indeed famous at lunch for crab cakes, cole slaw, and corn bread.

Capitol Hill/Northeast

Market Lunch, in Eastern Market, 225 7th St. SE (between 7th Street SE and North Carolina Avenue and C Street); (202) 547-8444; Tuesday-Saturday 6:30 a.m.-6:00 p.m.

Bread and Chocolate, 666 Pennsylvania Ave. SE; (202) 547-2875; Monday-Saturday 7:00 a.m.-7:30 p.m., Sunday 8:00 a.m.-6:30 p.m. (also three other D.C. locations and two Virginia locations). Metro Station: Eastern Market.

8 / Cultivate a Rich and Powerful Image: Part 1

Living It Up in D.C.

Everyone knows that Washington, D.C. is a city where image counts as much as substance. So here's a brief guide to looking and acting rich, powerful, hip, and chic.

Travel to D.C. Book first-class accommodations on the Metroliner (round trips, N.Y.C./D.C. $296). You get not only reserved seating and meal service, but also the perk of mingling with the other high rollers in Metropolitan Lounges, swanky '30s-style clublike hideaways inside stations in New York, D.C., Chicago, and Philadelphia.

Travel in D.C. Tour D.C. in a stretch limo with bar, TV, and stereo (about $75 per hour, including gratuity and taxes). Let everyone guess who's behind the tinted windows.

The Company You Keep Mingle with movie stars and rock musicians at the laid-back, luxurious Four Seasons 2800 Pennsylvania Ave. NW; (800) 322-3442. Your suite should overlook Rock Creek Park. Rub elbows with White House whizzes and deal-makers at the elegant Hay-Adams, 800 16th St. NW at H St.; (800) 424-5054. You have twenty-four-hour butler and maid service; your suite has a White House view. Hob-nob with sheiks and other heads of state at the understated Madison, 1177 15th St. NW; (800) 424-8577 or beaux arts Willard Inter-Continental, 1401 Pennsylvania Ave. NW at 14th St.; (800) 327-0200, where there are special security floors.

Your Stylist Cristophe—the Los Angeles-based celebrity hairdresser who brought traffic to a halt on an LAX tarmac when he trimmed President Clinton's hair aboard Air Force One—has a salon at 1125 18th St. NW; (202) 785-2222. He no longer cuts Clinton. But he will treat you like a VIP. He should—his haircuts cost $250, and for another $250, you can get a head-to-toe makeover. Cuppa coffee's free.

9 / Cultivate a Rich and Powerful Image: Part 2

More of the High Life

What You Wear—Top-of-the-Line Designer Fashions See Have a First-Class Secondhand Day (page 84).

Your Entertainment Time your trip to coincide with a National Theater opening night; Box 1 is reserved for the president. Book seats as close as possible to the center section, rows D-G, which usually are filled with political bigwigs and media moguls, 1321 Pennsylvania Ave. NW; (202) 628-6161. Metro Station: Metro Center.

Your Restaurants Drop $250 or more to dine à la carte with wine on multi-starred French food at Jean-Louis at the Watergate Hotel, 2650 Virginia Ave. NW; (202) 298-4488. Head to Galileo, 1110 21st St. NW; (202) 293-7191; for luxury-priced pasta in an evocative villa setting. Or, limo to the lovely Inn at Little Washington, in Washington, Virginia; Middle and Main streets; (703) 675-3800; for inspired New American cooking.

How You See the Sights Tour the city with private guide, Jean Fogle, a local historian who specializes in offbeat and little-known D.C. ($50 per hour).

Doing Tea Enjoy tea at the Four Seasons Hotel; the Hay-Adams; the Willard Inter-Continental (addresses on page 10); the Jefferson Hotel, 1200 16th St. NW; (800) 368-5966; the Ritz-Carlton, 2100 Massachusetts Ave. NW; (800) 241-3333; or the Henley Park (see page 53).

Where You Work Out Stretch and flex at the Watergate Club, Watergate Hotel, 2650 Virginia Ave. NW; (202) 965-2300; with political heavies (no pun intended) and film stars (daily fee: $20); or at the Washington Sports Club, 1835 Connecticut Ave. NW; (202) 332-0100; with younger, hipper Hill staffers.

Shuttle Etiquette Board at the last minute with an expensive briefcase and important look.

10 / Masterpiece of Urban Restoration

Union Station

These days, when you go to Union Station, you are heading for much more than your train. Union Station is also home to dozens of restaurants, numerous shops, and a nine-screen cineplex. Its successful renovation has given stunning new life to the railroad terminal and economic vitality to an entire neighborhood.

The beaux arts structure, built in the early 1900s by Daniel Burnham, was modeled after the baths and triumphal arches of ancient Rome. In 1937, at its peak, an estimated 42,000 people traversed the station's main concourse each day. After serving as the National Visitors' Center during the Bicentennial, the station closed in a grave state of decay. In 1981, a $160-million renovation put the station back on the right track.

When Union Station reopened in 1988, nearly every detail had been restored: original walls, windows, and scagliola (painted faux marble) columns, and even the IIII (instead of IV) in the big clock. The station's architectural triumph is its massive Main Hall, with its ninety-six-foot-high coffered ceiling accented with gold leaf, and thirty-six Roman legionnaires on the balcony.

Enjoy the grandeur in one of several restaurants in this hall, or snack below, where the fast-food shops are built into piers and arches reminiscent of the ancient Roman baths. The East Hall houses the station's most interesting shops, offering arts and crafts, antique watches, and unique jewelry. More shops line the tri-level Main Concourse. The Train Concourse connects with Amtrak and MARC trains, the cinema, and parking.

Capitol Hill/Northeast

Union Station, Massachusetts Avenue NE (between 1st and 2nd streets); (202) 289-1908. Station: Open twenty-four hours; information booth in Main Hall. Shops: Monday-Saturday 10 a.m.-9 p.m., Sunday noon-6 p.m. Restaurant hours vary. Metro Station: Union Station.

11 / Mind-expanding Afternoon

Black Heritage Tour

Think of the Lincoln Memorial, and familiar images of Henry Bacon's classical monument come to mind. But there is another, earlier Lincoln memorial—in the small nineteenth-century Lincoln Park, surrounded by turn-of-the-century houses, in southeast Washington, D.C.

This other Lincoln memorial—the Emancipation Memorial, sculpted in 1876 by Thomas Ball—is a life-size statue of President Lincoln holding the Emancipation Proclamation. At his feet is a slave, breaking his chains and beginning to stand. The sculptor modeled the slave's face after a photograph of Archer Alexander, the last person to be apprehended under the Fugitive Slave Act. This memorial was financed almost entirely by contributions from freed men and women.

In this same park is the impressive memorial to African-American educator-activist Mary McLeod Bethune. This memorial was both the first sculpture of a woman in a D.C. public park and the first in the District to honor an African American. Bethune, education advisor to FDR, was sculpted by African-American artist Robert Berks.

Lincoln Park is one stop on the mind-expanding Black Heritage Tour. Tour-goers also visit the Anacostia Museum and the impressive residence of Frederick Douglass (see page 19).

Among other landmarks on the tour is Benjamin Banneker Circle. Who was Banneker? Son of a former slave, this self-taught mathematician and astronomer helped Pierre Charles L'Enfant design the capital.

Capitol Hill/Northeast

Black Heritage Tour, Gray Line Tours, Union Station, bus level; (202) 289-1995. Departs 2 p.m., Wednesday and Saturday year-round; about four hours long. Adults $20; children $11. Reservations required. Metro Station: Union Station.

12 / See Your Government at Work

U.S. Capitol

The U.S. Capitol is Washington, D.C.'s grandest and most historic building. George Washington laid the cornerstone in 1793. Since then the building has been altered several times; in fact, it had to be rebuilt after the British torched it in 1814.

Thirty-minute tours begin in the Rotunda and take in the public areas. If you prefer, you can meander on your own, exploring the same route—Statuary Hall; the original Supreme Court Chamber; the Old Senate Chamber; and the Crypt, which was to be the tomb of George Washington. Statuary Hall is something of an acoustical curiosity: Stand above the bronze disc on the floor (marking the placement of John Quincy Adams' desk) and you can hear a whispered message from forty-five feet away.

If you wish to see government in action from the Visitors' Galleries in either the Senate or House, and you are not on a VIP tour (see page 1), pick up passes from your senator's or representative's Washington offices. Call (202) 224-3121 for office locations. Foreign visitors need only show their passports to enter the galleries.

American flags flying over their respective sides of the Capitol signal when the House and Senate are in session; a lantern in the dome means that at least one of the chambers is meeting.

To find out the Congressional schedule, call (202) 224-3121, or read the "Today in Congress" column in the *Washington Post*. This column also lists committee meetings that are open to the public. These are the pepper in government, and if you attend one, you may witness some hot discussion. To get to a House or Senate office building, take the special subway under the Capitol.

Capitol Hill/Northeast

U.S. Capitol, Capitol Hill (between Constitution and Independence avenues); (202) 225-6827 (tours). Tours daily, every fifteen minutes, 9 a.m.-3:45 p.m.; free. Metro Station: Capitol South or Union Station.

13 / Stamping Ground

National Postal Museum

The National Postal Museum, the fourteenth Smithsonian museum in Washington, D.C., isn't just for stamp enthusiasts, although it does house the world's largest collection of foreign and domestic stamps. Visit the museum and you will become engrossed with history in a way you never expected to be. The five galleries chiefly use documentary material—photographs, news clips, memorabilia, interactive video, and special games—to trace the evolution of the postal service from the colonists who carried mail over Indian trails to today's modern technology.

Through the magic of the latest interactive videos and other clever techniques, you can recall train wrecks and robberies and learn to detect mail fraud. Computers help you create a delivery route in the nineteenth century or carry the mail in a biplane.

"Moving the Mail," in the atrium, is the most dramatic display, with three delicate-looking early air-mail planes suspended from girders above a marble floor design of stamped envelopes. Here, too, are a railroad car and a stagecoach that earlier delivered mail.

One of the most touching scenes is in the exhibit "The Art of Cards and Letters." Here, an array of wartime correspondence artifacts and videos dramatize the sentiments expressed by soldiers and their loved ones in conflicts ranging from World War I to Operation Desert Storm. Catalogs from every era make up another colorful display. Photographs and memorabilia also chronicle the mail carriers' struggle for a living wage and decent hours (they once worked six days a week, with low pay and no vacations) and ultimately their move to unionize.

The museum occupies the lower level of the beaux arts City Post Office.

Capitol Hill/Northeast

National Postal Museum, corner of Massachusetts Avenue and First Street NE; information (202) 357-2700. Open daily 10:30 a.m.-5 p.m.; free. Metro Station: Union Station.

14 / Tops in Irish Life on Capitol Hill

Phoenix Park Hotel

If you are after a bit of Irish spirit, seek out several places across from Union Station that exude Celtic charm.

At the corner of Capitol and F streets NW, the eighty-seven-room Phoenix Park Hotel, named for the great greensward in the center of Dublin, adds the ambience of an eighteenth-century Irish country inn to Capitol Hill. While some rooms are leprechaun-size, they are full of amenities for guests: big wingback chairs, large beds, and well—stocked mini-bars.

On the second floor, the Powerscourt Restaurant is both elegant and intimate. Fellow diners might well include a famous politician or two. (Former Speaker Tip O'Neill's eightieth birthday bash took place here.) Chef Thomas Stack puts an amusing new spin on Irish cuisine: How about potato soup, garnished with lobster? A house favorite is sirloin steak seared with peppercorns, flamed with Irish whiskey, and finished with cream and tomatoes. Breakfast, lunch, and dinner served Monday-Friday; Saturday, dinner only; closed Sunday.

On the ground floor is The Dubliner, an authentic pub with live Irish bands at night. Lunch and dinner; Sunday breakfast.

A few steps up F Street, a Chinese pagoda mysteriously but charmingly houses The Irish Times, a restaurant decorated with owner Hugh Kelly's antiques and assorted bibelots. Ronald Reagan always dropped in here on St. Patrick's Day. Capitol Hill staffers regularly chow down here on such stick-to-the-ribs dishes as lamb stew and fish and chips at down-to-earth prices (three-course meal for two with beer, $25). Irish tunes on the juke box; live entertainment, Wednesday through Saturday. Lunch and dinner.

Capitol Hill/Northeast

Phoenix Park Hotel, 520 N. Capitol St. NW (at F St.); (202) 638-6900 and (800) 824-5419 (the hotel number, for restaurant reservations).

Irish Times, 14 F St. NW; (202) 543-5433. Metro Station: Union Station.

15 / Where Kids Can Be Kids

Capital Children's Museum

A garden full of fantastic animals and people created by folk artist Nek Chand welcomes you to the Capital Children's Museum. This garden is a miniature version of the multi-acre garden in Chand's home town of Chandigarh, India, and the only place in America you can see his work. Here, as in India, Chand recycles scrap metal, glass, tiles, and other castoffs to construct his fanciful Indian gardens.

If you're traveling with kids, this museum is a wonderful place to spend an hour or two. Unlike other museums, where kids are hushed, shushed, and told not to touch, this children's haven believes that learning begins with active participation. In this laboratory for growing minds, kids can putter, probe, and touch as much as they like. Grown-ups, too, are encouraged to twist the knobs and pull the gizmos that fascinate the youngsters.

The central idea at this museum is to learn by doing, which can mean trying anything from computing and cartooning to building and printing. Kids can send messages in Morse code, walk through a maze, slide through a mock-sewer pipe, and pretend to drive a fire engine or navigate traffic in a taxi or bus. Very young children squeal with delight as they hoist blocks with pulleys and levers, while those a little older enjoy exploring other cultures by trying on clothes, making crafts, and sampling foods.

Special educational exhibitions challenge children to learn new skills. A while back, Chuck Jones, the cartoonist whose creations include Bugs Bunny, was the subject of a show that taught children the intricate skills of animation. Another show helped children and grown-ups explore the world of the hearing impaired.

Capitol Hill/Northeast

Capital Children's Museum, 800 Third Ave. NE (between H and I streets); (202) 543-8600. Cost: $6 per person, free for kids 2 or younger. Daily, 10 a.m.-5 p.m. Crowded on weekends. Metro Station: Union Station.

16 / Witness High Court Rituals

U.S. Supreme Court

If the Supreme Court is in session, make every effort to hear a case being argued. For two weeks each month, Monday to Wednesday, the justices hear arguments. Cases on the docket are listed in the *Washington Post*'s "Supreme Court Calendar."

Arrive early; you must choose between two lines. The three- to five-minute line whisks you through for a quick view, and the longer line enables you to stay for the entire session. If you want the latter, be in line one to two hours early. (There are only 100-150 seats.)

Promptly at 10 a.m., the drama begins. All remain standing while the black-robed justices enter from behind parted red velvet drapes and the Court Marshall announces: "The Honorable, the chief Justice and Associate Justices of the Supreme Court of the United States."

While the justices are seated, the marshall continues: "Oyez, Oyez" (Hear Ye). "All persons having business before the Honorable, the Supreme Court of the United States, are admonished to draw near and give their attention, for the court is now sitting. God save the United States and this Honorable Court."

The Chief Justice sits in the center of the winged bench; to his right is the most senior justice. Ten-inch quill pens are placed on the lawyers' tables below the justices. After counsels present their thirty-minute arguments, their quills become souvenirs.

When the court is out of session, there's a lecture every hour on the half hour from 9:30 a.m. to 3:30 p.m. A film about the court is also shown.

Capitol Hill/Northeast

U.S. Supreme Court, First St. NE (between Maryland Avenue and E. Capitol Street); (202) 479-3030. Court, Monday-Friday 9 a.m.-4:30 p.m. Cafeteria, Monday-Friday 7:30-10:30 a.m., 11:30 a.m.-noon; 12:15-1 p.m.,1:15-2 p.m. Metro Station: Capitol South or Union Station.

17 / First Official U.S. Monument to an African American

Frederick Douglass National Historic Site (Cedar Hill)

Welcome to the first official U.S. monument honoring an African American—Cedar Hill, the home of Frederick Douglass, fugitive slave turned abolitionist leader. Perched high above the city, the three-story, twenty-one-room white Victorian house, built in 1854, was originally off-limits to any person of African blood. But the racial barrier was broken and Douglass bought this home in 1877 for $6,700. He lived here until 1895, when he died on the premises of a heart attack. The house is maintained by the National Park Service, which guides the tours.

Before touring the house, take a moment on the spacious porch to admire the wonderful view of Washington, D.C. and surrounding area.

Douglass, born a slave in 1817 and taught to read and write by his master's wife, escaped to Massachusetts at 21. He became a powerful abolitionist orator and an adviser to President Lincoln, urging him to enlist blacks in the Union Army. Later, he supported the Republican platform for black suffrage.

Most of the furnishings at Cedar Hill are original. Among the mementos in the house are a cane and other gifts from Abraham Lincoln. Visitors see the Victorian parlor and bedrooms, old-fashioned kitchen, dining room, and Douglass's personal library with the 1,200 volumes that were his most treasured possessions.

The Visitor Center, at the base of the hill, shows a short film portrait of Douglass. The center also displays a life-size statue of Douglass; Douglass's death mask; and a copy of *North Stars*, the newspaper Douglass edited in 1849.

Anacostia/Southeast

Frederick Douglass National Historic Site, 1411 W St. SW (between 14th and 15th streets); (202) 426-5960. Open daily; free. No nearby Metro Station; on Gray Line and Tourmobile routes. Not a great neighborhood to wander in; take the tour.

18 / Classic First Stop for Museum-goers

The Castle

When confused tourists start asking questions about the fourteen museums and galleries (and the zoo!) of the Smithsonian Institution, they're likely to get a version of the old movie line: "Yonder is da Castle. . . ." Why? Because The Castle, otherwise known as the Smithsonian Institute Building, is the place to go for information about all parts of the Smithsonian.

Architecturally, this red sandstone Gothic Revival fantasy with turrets, towers, and crenellations is one of the city's more offbeat landmarks. Completed in 1855, it houses the Smithsonian's Information Center. Visitors can pick up maps and brochures, and view a short film of Smithsonian highlights.

James Smithson (1765-1829), a British scientist, was the founder of the Smithsonian Institution. Smithson had named his nephew as his beneficiary, unless that nephew failed to produce an heir. When that nephew died childless in 1835, Smithson's inheritance, in accordance with the terms of Smithson's will, went to the United States to found "at Washington, an establishment under the name of Smithsonian Institution, for the increase and diffusion of knowledge among men." Smithson's fortune, amounting to $500,000 in gold sovereigns (big bucks then), was shipped in sacks to the United States. Smithson himself had never set foot in America.

Smithson, an illegitimate son of a duke and descendant of Henry VII, distinguished himself as a scientist but was never fully accepted in his native England because of his birth. His tomb is in the Crypt Room to the left of the Castle's entrance.

Southwest/The Mall

The Castle, 1000 Jefferson Dr. SW (at 10th Street); (202) 357-2700. Open 9 a.m.-5 p.m. daily; free. Metro Station: Smithsonian.

19 / View Points

Prime Perches for Sunsets

A brilliant sunset from a perch above the city can be a perfect ending to any day. Here are several recommended vantage points from which to choose.

On the Mall, no view surpasses the panorama from the Washington Monument. At a height of 555 feet, you take in all of the surrounding area as the sun sets and the city's lights flicker on. But you may have to queue up for this view. For several splendid sunset views in less hectic surroundings, cross the Potomac to northern Virginia and head for one of the following perches.

The seventy-eight-foot-high Marine Corps War Memorial provides perhaps the ultimate sunset experience when it comes to catching the last rays on the Mall's landmarks. Come early to explore the bronze statue that shows the raising of the flag at Iwo Jima. Metro Station: Rosslyn or Arlington Cemetery.

Nearby is the Netherlands Carillon, a gift to the United States from the people of Holland. Visitors are permitted into the tower to admire the view and watch the carillonneur perform. In Arlington Cemetery, the grave site of Pierre Charles L'Enfant is a sunset spot: The D.C. designer's resting place appropriately offers a grand city view. Metro Station: Arlington Cemetery.

Another Arlington choice is The View, an upscale restaurant (jacket/tie/reservations) atop the Key Bridge Marriott, 1401 Lee Hwy., Arlington, Virginia; (703) 524-6400. From here, the views of Georgetown and all of D.C. are a knockout! The glass-enclosed Vantage Point restaurant, Best Western Rosslyn Westpark Hotel, 1900 N. Ft. Myer Dr., is tops at sunset. Reservations recommended; (703) 527-4814. Metro Station for both: Rosslyn.

Back in Washington: Steps from the Mall, at the outdoor rooftop bar at the Hotel Washington, 515 15th St. NW; (202) 638-5900; sunset is served with cocktails and a view of the White House gardens. Metro Station: Metro Center.

Southwest/The Mall

20 / Double Your Pleasure

Cherry Blossoms and Tulips

Springtime in Washington, D.C., when the Tidal Basin is awash with cherry trees doing their thing, is a popular sight; no two ways about it. Too popular, in fact. People flood the city to catch a glimpse, and the resulting gridlock is akin to that at Rockefeller Center when the Christmas tree is on display. Few look beyond the cherry trees. A pity.

Within a whiff of the blossoms is another floral spectacle many Washingtonians seem unaware of—the marvelous "tulip library." Double your pleasure and see both the cherry blossoms and tulips.

More than ten thousand tulip bulbs are planted each year by the National Park Service, near the Tidal Basin between Independence Avenue and Raoul Wallenberg Place (formerly 15th Street NW). Around the first week in April, the tide of color bursts and floods the area near the Tidal Basin, between the Washington Monument and the Jefferson Memorial. This open-air treasury of Dutch tulips is replaced with the hues of other annuals when the tulips no longer are in bloom, making the area welcoming to visitors through the summer and fall.

By tulip time, the cherry trees should be in full bloom, having started around March 10. Sometimes they bloom as late as mid-April. With or without their pinkish-white blossoms, the annual Cherry Blossom Festival begins the first week in April. The hoopla begins with the lighting of the Mall's Japanese Lantern, then continues for seven days with parades, pageants, concerts, and a marathon.

The city's three thousand cherry trees were a gift from Japan in 1912; the hundreds of blooming trees in Potomac Park around the Tidal Basin are the most renowned. Walk from the Metro's Smithsonian station.

Southwest

21 / Go Underground: Part 1

National Museum of African Art

What's happening underground in Washington, D.C.? Two great choices in museums are side-by-side underground: the National Museum of African Art and the Sackler Gallery, dedicated to Asian art (see page 24). To conserve space, the Smithsonian slipped the museums into triangular spaces below the 4.2-acre Enid Haupt Garden.

The only museum in America dedicated to the artistic heritage of Africa, the National Museum of African Art started in a row of houses in 1964. It became part of the Smithsonian in 1979 and has been in its current building since 1987.

The museum is committed to showing how the continent's nine hundred distinct cultures make art an intrinsic part of all aspects of daily life. To many people who think of African art mainly as masks and wood figures, this museum is an eye- and mind-opener.

Holdings include a fine collection of royal Benin (Nigerian) art, as well as an array of utilitarian objects from other localities, such as stools, headrests, baskets, and ceramics.

On the first level, the exhibitions are drawn from the museum's ever-expanding permanent collection. Here are galleries showing sculpture from various geographic areas of Africa; pottery, accompanied by an excellent video; and personal objects of exceptional beauty, mainly from eastern and southern Africa, such as pipes, bowls, spoons, and potlids. The second level houses a twenty-thousand-volume library on African art.

Some of the museum's most engaging programs—such as folk story-telling and mask-making—are aimed at families and children.

Southwest/The Mall

National Museum of African Art, 950 Independence Ave. SW; information, (202) 357-2020; weekend tours and events, (202) 357-2700. Open 10 a.m.-5:30 p.m. every day except December 25; free. Library by appointment. Shop. Metro Station: Smithsonian.

22 / Go Underground: Part 2

Arthur M. Sackler Gallery

This Smithsonian museum is an underground treasury for Arthur M. Sackler's collection of Asian art. Sackler, a wealthy New York medical researcher, psychiatrist, and publisher, asked the curators of the Smithsonian to select one thousand items from his Asian art collection and donated four million dollars for the construction of a museum. The museum opened in 1987, with the Sackler works as its core, and has added other acquisitions since then.

On exhibit are Chinese works from the Shang (1766-1122 B.C.) to the Han (202 B.C.-A.D. 220) dynasties; more than 400 Chinese jades from 3000 B.C. to the twentieth century; and 156 Near Eastern objects in bronze, gold, and other mediums. Works from India, Thailand, and Indonesia also are part of the collection.

The first-level exhibits include Indian and Persian paintings, and Chinese Ming dynasty furniture. Among the most fascinating exhibits on this level are displays of Shang dynasty objects with animal motifs. These objects, used for state and religious rituals, show an extraordinary level of sophistication in design.

The second level at the Sackler is devoted to Chinese bronzes and neolithic jades, some from the fourth millennium B.C. On this level also is the thirty-five-thousand-volume library, half in either Chinese or Japanese.

The Sackler and the neighboring Freer Gallery are connected by a lower-level passageway and elevators. The galleries share the Meyer Auditorium, where lectures and performing arts programs are presented. Among the most intriguing programs are daily in-depth discussions at noon, when curators highlight specific objects from the collections.

Southwest/The Mall

Arthur M. Sackler Gallery, 1050 Independence Ave. SW; (202) 357-2700. Open 10 a.m.-5:30 p.m. daily; free. Tours; evening hours for some programs. Metro Station: Smithsonian.

23 / Great Freebies and Discounts
Budget Entertainment

Smithsonian   They say it would take eight to ten years to go through all the Smithsonian museums if you spent ten minutes at each exhibit. Stay as long as you wish; they're all free. For specifics, visit the Information Center at the Smithsonian Institution Building (see page 20). Metro Station: Smithsonian.

Discounted Tix   Half-price tickets (cash only) go on sale the day of the show for performances at the Kennedy Center, Arena Stage, and National and Warner theaters at TicketPlace, F Street Plaza, between 12th and 13th streets NW. Information: (202) 842-5387. Metro Station: Metro Center.

Library of Congress   Free chamber music concerts (202) 707-5502; poetry readings (202) 707-5394; vintage films (202) 707-5677; and lectures and symposia (202) 707-8000 year-round. Events calendars at the information counter in the Madison Building, 101 Independence Ave. SE. Metro Station: Capitol South or Union Station.

National Academy of Sciences   Free chamber music concerts by famous artists, October-May, 2101 Constitution Ave. NW; (202) 334-2436. Metro Station: Foggy Bottom.

Sylvan Theater   Free military and big band concerts every Sunday and Tuesday through Friday at 8 p.m., Memorial Day-Labor Day. On the grounds of the Washington Monument, 15th St. SW at Jefferson Dr. SW. Metro Station: Smithsonian.

Carter Barron Amphitheater   Free; everything from salsa to Shakespeare is presented from mid-June through August at the 4,250-seat outdoor theater. Rock Creek Park at 16th St. and Colorado Ave. NW; (202) 426-6837 or (202) 619-7222 off season.

Military Parades and Drills   Free Friday at 8 p.m. at the Marine Corps Barracks, mid-May through early September. At 8th St. SE between G and I streets; (202) 433-6060. Reserve three weeks in advance. Metro Station: Eastern Market.

Southwest/The Mall

24 / In the Memory of Millions

United States Holocaust Memorial Museum

The United States Holocaust Memorial is a museum and memorial all in one and like no other. Opened in 1993, it already has become one of the most moving tributes in a city renowned for remarkable monuments. Plan to spend at least one-half day here.

The architect James I. Freed, who escaped Germany in 1939, uses such features as narrow passageways, slanted walls, and off-kilter staircases to symbolize the strangely insane world of the Nazi regime. The mammoth Hall of Witness calls to mind a surreal European train station. From here, visitors ascend by elevator to the permanent exhibition. Through authentic relics, eyewitness testimony, photographs, films, graphics, and music, visitors learn how Nazi fanaticism resulted in the deaths of six million Jews and millions of other victims. Displays also tell of heroic rescues by resistors and of the anger at America's failure to bomb Auschwitz.

The exhibits are heart-breaking: a room full of shoes left behind by the dead; a three-story tower with more than one thousand photographs of a nine-hundred-year-old Jewish community that was destroyed in two days by the Nazis; a railroad freight car that transported people to death camps; and other exhibits, one after another, that purposely build disturbing images viewers will never forget.

The Hall of Remembrance, a six-sided chamber with a skylight, was created as a place for reflection and formal ceremonies.

The Children's Wall of Remembrance honors the one-and-a-half-million children murdered by the Nazis; it features handpainted tiles made by American schoolchildren. Another exhibit, "Remembering the Children: Daniel's Story," explains the Holocaust to youngsters.

Southwest/The Mall

United States Holocaust Memorial Museum, 100 Raoul Wallenberg Pl. SW; (202) 488-0400. Open daily, 10 a.m.-5:30 p.m.; free. Metro Station: Smithsonian.

25 / Make a Fantastic Voyage

National Air and Space Museum

It's no wonder the National Air and Space Museum is the most popular museum in D.C. (with an estimated eight million visitors annually) and perhaps the world: It is actually one of the most remarkable. If you had only one day to visit in Washington, D.C., the early hours should be spent here, the middle hours at a beautiful garden, the late afternoon at the American Museum of Natural History, the sunset at the Old Post Office Pavilion tower (or another viewpoint), and the evening at a satiric review. These together wrap up much of our world, roots, natural beauty, stages of development, and future, as well as political foibles.

As is true of all great museums, the National Air and Space Museum cannot be absorbed in one visit, nor completely described in this brief write-up. Yet even the lightest skimming of the displays, from the earliest plane to the space shuttles, provides an understanding of how flight has changed our lives, as a way to travel, trade, communicate, see, and explore the world today.

Before you start exploring the twenty-three galleries that trace the history of flight, take a minute to plot a route. If you're with kids, they'll be drawn to the interactive exhibits; you can touch the Mercury spacecraft, *Friendship 7* (in which John Glenn became the first American to circle the earth), as well as a moon rock; see simulated landings on an aircraft landing deck; walk through Skylab; and admire all manner of planes and early rockets.

To many, the museum theater's special projection system will provide the most memorable thrills. The mammoth IMAX projection system with five-story screen makes viewers feel part of the action.

Southwest/The Mall

National Air and Space Museum, Independence Ave. at 6th St. SW; (202) 357-2700. Open daily, June 14-Labor Day, 10 a.m.-6:30 p.m.; rest of the year, 10 a.m.-5:30 p.m.; free. Three gift shops, cafeteria, restaurant, bar. Metro Station: L'Enfant Plaza (Smithsonian exit).

26 / A Powerful Symbol of Remembrance

Vietnam Veterans Memorial

The striking black granite Vietnam Veterans Memorial with its finely engraved list of more than fifty-eight thousand casualties may be an archetypal symbol of remembrance. Since its dedication in 1982, it has become one of the most visited sites in Washington, D.C. and one of the nation's most moving antiwar memorials.

Veterans' groups regularly pay tribute at the wall, as do civilians who suffered losses. Volunteers help visitors make tracings of names on the walls. Many visitors leave letters, flowers, medals, and photos—touching tokens of remembrance. The National Park Service is preserving these gifts.

Congress authorized the memorial's construction in 1980 and held a national competition for its design. The unanimous choice from 1,421 entries was the design submitted by Maya Ying Lin, then a twenty-one-year-old Yale graduate student.

The memorial's two walls, each 246 feet, 8 inches long, are angled toward the Washington Monument and Lincoln Memorial as if to embrace past history. Names of those killed or unaccounted for are listed in the order they became casualties, beginning at the walls' intersection. Directories at the entrance and exit list the names alphabetically.

Lin's stark wall is extremely unconventional for a war memorial. Now universally admired and accepted, it initially created controversy. Soon after its completion, a flagpole and bronze sculpture of three soldiers by Frederick Hart were placed nearby to please traditionalists. More recently, Glenna Goodacre's Vietnam Woman's Memorial was added to the site to honor the ten thousand women who served in the war. *Southwest/The Mall*

Vietnam Veterans Memorial, Constitution Gardens, near Lincoln Memorial (between 21st and 22nd streets NW); (202) 634-1568, for information. Open twenty-four hours; staffed 8 a.m.-midnight. Metro Station: Foggy Bottom or Smithsonian..

27 / Scandalmongers
Gross National Product

If you see no humor in an HMO, here's one that will keep you in stitches. Gross National Product, the longest-running satirical troupe in Washington, D.C., recommends large doses of HMO (Humor Maintenance Organization) every day for what ails you.

The troupe, which media critics have dubbed the hottest comedy troupe in D.C., dishes out a double scoop of wicked fun: they perform at the Arena Stage and also run "Scandal Tours" to places that have put Washington, D.C. on the infamous map.

First, about the Arena Stage act: a recent GNP show "A Newt World Order" skewered the Republicans. Earlier, with "Clintoons," GNP made fun of Democrats in general and such tasty targets as Dan Rostenkowski in particular. Famous figures—including Rush Limbaugh—get roasted; so do American industries such as tobacco (in a sketch titled "The R. J. Reynolds Museum of Tobacco and Smoking") and entertainment ("Walt Dismal's America").

Then there are GNP's witty, irreverent guided tours of the sites that have made Washington, D.C. the scandal capital of the world. Stops include the White House, where GNP discovers skeletons from way back in the closet; the Tidal Basin, site of the moonlight swim of Wilbur Mills and Fanny Fox; Gary Hart's town house; Watergate naturally, and many, many more. Aboard the tour bus, members of the troupe dramatize D.C.'s sleazier side.

For those who want to scandalize themselves, GNP offers a Scandal-Tour-in-a-Box cassette, which comes with classified shreddings and the Official Scandal Tour Map. *Southwest*

Gross National Product, at the Arena Stage, 6th St. and Main Ave. SW; (202) 488-3300. Fridays at 9 p.m. and Saturdays at 8 and 10 p.m. Tickets $18; cabaret setting, drinks served. Metro Station: Waterfront.

Scandal Tours, Saturdays, 1 p.m., Memorial Day-Labor Day. Tickets $27; reservations required; (202) 783-7212.

Tour-in-a-Box, $12.95; to order, call (301) 587-4291.

28 / Time to Sniff the Posies

U.S. Botanic and Enid A. Haupt Gardens

At 175 years old, the U.S. Botanic Garden is the oldest continually operating botanic garden in the country. The gardens between the Capitol and the Mall are in nineteenth-century iron-and-glass houses that would have brought a smile to Queen Victoria's lips. Each little house stars a rare species: cacti, ferns, tropicals. Seasonal shows feature tulips in spring, chrysanthemums in fall, and poinsettias in winter.

The gardens include Bartholdi Park, with a handsome cast-iron fountain by Frédéric Auguste Bartholdi, designer of the Statue of Liberty. Here, mythological figures represent the elements of light and water.

Picnic on the terrace at an umbrella-shaded table with a view of the Capitol. Slated to open in five to six years in this area is a new National Garden with a learning center.

For another botanical blast from the past, stroll along the Mall to the ground-level garden that crowns the underground National Museum of African Art and Arthur M. Sackler Gallery. Although the Enid A. Haupt Garden was created recently, the 1870s cast-iron benches and turn-of-the-century-type lamp posts and floral designs give this garden a distinctive old-fashioned look and feel. The Independence Street entrance has elaborate cast-iron gates to blend with the Victorian-era Castle. No picnics here.

Southwest/The Mall

U.S. Botanic Garden, 245 First St. SW (between Independence and Maryland avenues); (202) 225-8333. Open daily 9 a.m.-5 p.m., September-May; daily 9 a.m.-9 p.m. June-August; free. Metro Station: Federal Center.

Enid A. Haupt Garden, between Independence and Maryland avenues; (202) 357-2700. Open Memorial Day-Labor Day, 7 a.m.- 8 p.m.; 7 a.m.-5:45 p.m. remainder of year; closed December 25; free. Metro Station: Smithsonian.

29 / Those Other Washington Monuments

Public Figures (in Private Places)

You've seen the presidential memorials on the Mall; now here are a few places to look at live pols and other famous people.

For a chance to see Bill Clinton, rise early and run to East and West Potomac parks, where he sometimes jogs. You'll know when he's there by his entourage of TV trucks and Secret Service agents. Try some '90s-lifestyle restaurants. The Clintons' visit brought increased fame to Nora's organic-based cuisine, 2132 Florida Ave. NW; (202) 462-5143; Metro Station: Dupont Circle.

Hip young Clintonites unwind after work in Shaw, in the Northwest sector. Visit Andalusian Dog, 1344 U St. NW; (202) 986-6364; with Daliesque melting watch decor, where they deliberate over tapas. Also check out State of the Union, 1357 U St. NW; (202) 588-8810; where the Russian ambience carries through to the tiled bar with twenty different Russian vodkas plus a few house flavors. No balalaikas, but the latest in jazz. (Metro Station for both: U St.-Cardozo; at night, take a taxi.)

Denzel Washington and Jesse Jackson are fans of the South Carolina Low Country cuisine at Georgia Brown's Square, 1500 K St. NW; (202) 393-4499; Metro Station: McPherson Square (see page 39).

The Jockey Club, Ritz-Carlton Hotel, 2100 Massachusetts Ave. NW; (202) 659-8000; Metro Station: Dupont Circle; has long been popular with celebs such as humorist Art Buchwald, TV news anchor Barbara Walters, and TV newscaster Peter Arnett (CNN). Many big-name politicians like the steaks at Sam & Harry's, 1200 19th St. NW; (202) 296-4333; Metro Station: Dupont Circle.

Stroll Georgetown, for sightings of the rich and famous in their own habitat.

Not intimate enough? To see George Stephanopolous in shorts, check out the Stairmasters at the rear of the Washington Sports Club, 1835 Connecticut Ave. NW; (202) 332-0100; daily fee $20; Metro Station: Dupont Circle. *Southwest*

30 / Smart Tours for Kids

Museums, Monuments, and Breaks In Between

Start at the Smithsonian Castle to check out the exhibits and activities specially tailored to kids (see page 20). Experience at least one of these. Metro Station: Smithsonian.

See crime labs, confiscated loot, and marksmanship demonstrations: Federal Bureau of Investigation, 10th St. and Pennsylvania Ave. NW; tour entrance on E St. NW; (202) 324-3447; open 8:45 a.m.-4:15 p.m.; closed federal holidays. Metro Station: Federal Triangle or Archives-Navy Memorial.

Watch billions of dollars roll off the presses: Bureau of Engraving and Printing, 14th and C streets SW; (202) 874-3019; Monday-Friday 9 a.m.-2 p.m. Metro Station: Smithsonian.

Pedalboat on the Tidal Basin while admiring the Jefferson Memorial. The pier is northeast of the Memorial.

Explore Flora Gill Jacob's treasury of antique dolls and toys: Washington Dolls' House and Toy Museum, 5236 44th St. NW, between Harrison and Jennifer streets; (202) 244-0024; Tuesday-Saturday, 10 a.m.-5 p.m.; Sunday, noon-5 p.m. Adults $3, children under fourteen, $1. Metro Station: Friendship Heights.

Hold a creature or two at the Insect Zoo; sniff, touch, and taste natural history specimens in the Discovery Room: National Museum of Natural History, Madison Dr. NW between 9th and 12th streets; (202) 357-2700; open daily 10:30 a.m.-5:30 p.m.; closed December 25. Discovery Room open weekdays noon-2:30 p.m.; Friday-Sunday 10:30 a.m.-3:30 p.m. Metro Station: Smithsonian.

Ride an old-fashioned carousel in summer: near the Arts and Industries Building, Jefferson Dr. and 9th St. NW. Metro Station: Smithsonian.

Take a seventy-second ride up and a "Walking Down the Steps Tour" back down to learn the inside story of the Washington Monument; call the National Park Service (202) 426-6840, for step-down tour schedules. Metro Station: Smithsonian.

31 / World-renowned East-Meets-West Collection

Freer Gallery of Art

The Freer Gallery houses world-renowned Asian art and nineteenth- and twentieth-century American art collections. It also has the world's single most important collection of works by the American artist James McNeill Whistler.

The Freer opened in 1923 as the Smithsonian's first fine arts museum. The core of the collection was amassed by Detroit industrialist Charles Lang Freer (1854-1919). Freer approved the museum's Italian Renaissance design, which places nineteen galleries around a lovely courtyard.

Freer began by collecting American art; his first Asian acquisition was a fan. The aesthetic interests of the artist Whistler, a close friend, inspired Freer's involvement with Asian art. He saw a distinct visual relationship between his American and Asian acquisitions. For art lovers, his collection is a rare opportunity to study the interdependence of these two traditions.

The museum's exhibits are drawn entirely from its own reserves. Freer said that no American works could be added to his collection, but placed no restrictions on the Asian portion. Currently, the twenty-seven thousand objects in the Freer collection span four millennia and include collections of ancient bronzes, jades, and porcelains; Korean stoneware; Buddhist sculptures; Chinese paintings; Japanese paper screens; and Islamic art.

Gallery 12 holds "The Peacock Room." Whistler designed this dining room for an English shipping magnate as a backdrop to the artist's painting *Princess from the Land of Porcelain*. Freer paid $30,000 for the room and shipped it to America.

A twenty-six-million dollar, five-year renovation of the Freer was completed in 1993. *Southwest*

Freer Gallery of Art, Jefferson Drive SW at 12th St.; (202) 357-2700. Open daily except December 25, 10 a.m.-5:30 p.m. Shop. Metro Station: Smithsonian.

32 / Attend a Gala

John F. Kennedy Center for the Performing Arts

On Washington's social landscape, the Kennedy Center Honors is an Everest. All society turns out for this glittering fund raiser recognizing lifetime achievement in the arts. You can, too, if you pay as much as five thousand dollars for your ticket.

The people who keep our country going are there, as are their powerful friends. Columnists and photographers are there, sniffing around for quotes and photo ops. There is a lot of milling about, sipping champagne in the Grand Foyer, beneath the eighteen sparkling Orrefors crystal chandeliers (a gift from Sweden) and the reception area for the three main theaters—the concert hall, opera house, and Eisenhower Theater for plays and small musical productions.

Feel Lilliputian in the foyer? It's not the bubbly. At 630 feet by 40 feet, this is one of the world's largest rooms. In the foyer is the bronze bust of John F. Kennedy, who is memorialized here. To either side are the Hall of States, flying the flags of our states, D.C., and territories; and the Hall of Nations, with flags of the countries with which we have diplomatic relations.

All the theaters have presidential boxes. When the president attends a performance such as the Kennedy Center Honors, his seal is placed on the front of his box.

There are private dinner parties before the gala. But you can dine at the Rooftop Terrace restaurant, where both the view and pre-opening dinner deserve bravos.

Can't make it to the Honors? Don't miss the Kennedy Center. Be sure to take a daily tour, 10 a.m.-1 p.m., and attend some other event where you can dress down while living it up.

Foggy Bottom/West End

John F. Kennedy Center for the Performing Arts, New Hampshire Ave. NW at Rock Creek Parkway NW; information (202) 416-8341; to charge tickets, (202) 467-4600. Metro Station: Foggy Bottom.

33 / Go Behind the Scenes at the State Department

Diplomatic Reception Rooms

The elegant Diplomatic Reception Rooms on the eighth floor of the State Department building, filled with eighteenth- and nineteenth-century antiques, make you feel you've stepped off the elevator into an earlier era.

When the building opened in 1961, it was a different story. The first gala in the new reception rooms was to be for a visiting king, and when the wife of the then-Secretary of State saw them, they say, she wept. The rooms were furnished in mundane modern.

Clement Conger, then-chief of protocol in charge of diplomatic functions, came to the rescue. Conger took over the task of furnishing the rooms. He was inspired by both the grand European halls and gracious colonial American plantations. The rooms' pieces themselves, acquired through donations, now comprise one of the world's most notable collections of American antiques.

Forty-five-minute tours of three rooms are conducted for small groups; they must be booked well in advance.

The extraordinarily handsome John Quincy Adams State Drawing Room has the Treaty of Paris desk (1783) with treaty copy signed by Adams, John Jay, and Benjamin Franklin. Here, too, is Thomas Jefferson's desk, where it is believed he drafted the Declaration of Independence. To accommodate contemporary gatherings, the Benjamin Franklin State Dining Room is larger than any typical room in the Colonial era. Franklin memorabilia here includes his watch and watchstand, busts by Houdon, and a portrait painted in 1758.

Foggy Bottom/West End

Diplomatic Reception Rooms (State Department), C and 22nd sts. NW (between 21st and 23rd streets); (202) 647-3241. Tours Monday-Friday 9:30 and 10:30 a.m., 2:45 p.m. Free. Reservations required four weeks in advance. No strollers; not recommended for children under twelve. Photo I.D. required. Metro Station: Foggy Bottom and a five-block walk.

34 / Old-Fashioned Values Meet Today's Realities

The Corcoran Gallery of Art

There's the elegant foyer and remarkable American and European portraits and landscapes. There's the Duc de la Tremouille's incredible eighteenth-century French furniture. So far, nothing to irritate Jesse Helms. In fact, the Corcoran seems in perfect conservative taste. But how wrong can you be? The Corcoran is also on the cutting edge: It was the Corcoran's Mapplethorpe exhibit that led to Helms's attack on NEA grants. The Corcoran is a must-see.

It is also a school, an active supporter of local artists, and a showcase for varied special exhibits. Plus there's the Corcoran's café in the spacious atrium, which rates rave reviews from finicky critics, and the gospel brunches that rock the rafters every Sunday.

The privately funded gallery, which occupies a prime chunk of real estate within steps of the White House, was founded in 1869 by banker/philanthropist William Wilson Corcoran. He commissioned Ernest Flagg to design this beaux arts building to house his private collection. The Corcoran opened in 1897.

You can't do justice to it all in one visit. Pick up a map at the entrance, and make preliminary selections.

The American collection is seen selectively on the second floor. This assemblage of three thousand paintings, ranging from the colonial period to the twentieth century, includes portraiture, landscapes, and historical pictures.

The Senator William A. Clark and Edward C. and Mary Walker collections of fine European and decorative arts from the fifteenth to nineteenth centuries are on the first floor. Special exhibits are on both floors. *Foggy Bottom/West End*

The Corcoran Gallery of Art, 500 17th St. NW (corner of New York Ave.); (202) 638-3211; Wednesday-Monday, 10 a.m.-5 p.m.; Thursday, 10 a.m.-9 p.m.; closed Tuesday. Café, shop. Admission $3 adults; children under twelve free. Metro Station: Farragut West.

35 / Paris on the Potomac
Palladin

Don't go to famous chef Jean-Louis Palladin's new namesake bistro at the Watergate (also home to his renowned restaurant, Jean-Louis) expecting humdrum dishes such as boeuf bourguignonne. His is a refreshingly distinctive version of bistro fare: How about farm-raised squab pot-au-feu with cheese ravioli? On weekends there's such demand that they run out of this and other popular selections, but you won't be unhappy settling for alternatives. Just make reservations days in advance or you won't get in.

The best tables at Palladin are adjacent to the ceiling-to-floor windows; with the Potomac rolling by, you feel you're on a classy yacht. Graceful Roman-striped chairs, mellow woods, abundant fresh flowers, and snowy linens give this bistro an upscale look, and patrons dress up when eating here.

Busy yourself with the complimentary pastrami salmon with peppery crust and pâté while studying the ambitious and interesting menu and well-thought-out wine list. Memorable starters might include pine-nut-studded vegetable tartare in a puddle of tomato coulis, or white and green asparagus with sauce maltaise (blood oranges and hollandaise). Follow this with an entrée of moist roast Muscovy duck spiked with a piquant lime sauce; or a tasty fresh turbot in an elegant potato crust with tomato mirepoix, olives, and lemon confit. Desserts—worth a week's calories—change daily, but might include floating island and chocolate praline mousse crunch.

Palladin also offers an adventurous gourmet menu (requiring twenty-four hours notice) for fricassee of snails with mushrooms, garlic, and lemon grass, and two dozen other dishes.

Foggy Bottom/West End

Palladin (Watergate Hotel), 2650 Virginia Ave. NW ; (202) 298-4455. Open daily; breakfast, 7-10:30 a.m.; lunch, 11:30 a.m.-2:30 p.m.; dinner, 5:30-10:30 p.m. Reservations essential. Metro Station: Foggy Bottom.

36 / Toute Suite

State Plaza/Canterbury Hotel

Affordable suites? Yes, indeed. Here are two wonderful buys (especially on weekends and off-season) in intimate all-suite hotel hideaways in fashionable neighborhoods.

Tucked away on a tree-lined street, the State Plaza's lobby is furnished with antiques and accented by lovely plants and floral arrangements. The spacious suites carry through the antique look with period beds and chests, potted palms, and botanical prints on the walls. Each suite has a kitchen, dining area, mini-bar, cable TV, and well-appointed bathrooms. The hotel has a grocery shopping service (stores nearby for do-it-yourselfers) and coin-op laundry. The State Plaza is popular with both State Department guests and Kennedy Center performers.

The Garden Café has Federalist-inspired decor, an adjoining outdoor terrace, and critically acclaimed New American cuisine. Even if you choose to stay elsewhere, try to get to the café for a meal.

Discreet and elegant, the Canterbury Hotel is near the chic shops in Dupont Circle. Each suite has a sitting area, dressing room, kitchenette, restful color scheme, period reproduction furnishings, and a pleasantly cozy look; TVs have HBO hookups. Bathrooms have hair dryers and telephones. A complimentary welcome cocktail and continental breakfast are perks.

The hotel's wood-paneled Chaucer room, serving continental cuisine, is another plus. At the English-theme Union Jack Pub, there are the requisite dart board, fish and chips, and other typical tidbits, as well as English beers on tap. It draws a lively local crowd, and is a fun place to visit even if you stay elsewhere.

State Plaza, 2117 E St. NW; (202) 861-8200, (800) 424-2859. Metro Station: Foggy Bottom

Canterbury Hotel, 1733 N St. NW; (202) 393-3000, (800) 424-2950. Metro Station: Dupont Circle. Foggy Bottom/West End

37 / Come and Git 'Em: Haute Grits

Georgia Brown's

While there are fried green tomatoes on the menu, this is no Whistlestop Café. Georgia Brown's takes soul food from quaint and regional to upscale and cosmopolitan.

The setting is a stylized garden with trailing metal kudzu vines overhead, rounded banquettes, and mellow woods; the food, a blend of settlers' cuisines dating back three hundred years.

Here's the story: In the seventeenth century, all land south of Virginia from Pawley's Island to the Savannah River and inland as far as Charleston was "Low Country." This bountiful area was especially attractive to French Huguenots, Sephardic Jews, and settlers from West Africa. Their three distinct culinary traditions, melded with local favorites, produced a special soul-satisfying Low Country cuisine. This cuisine, updated by Chef Terrell Danby, is the mainstay of Georgia Brown's.

While studying the menu's beguiling selections, nibble the tongue-teasing Tabasco-cheddar crackers that the waiters bring you. The fare is an eclectic mix. It features Southern staples such as fried chicken with mashed potatoes; pork chops with collards and black-eyed peas; grits; and smoked bacon greens. Yet it includes haute creations such as head-on white shrimp with river clams and fresh mussels over red rice with spicy sausage gravy; and braised rabbit with wild mushrooms and rosemary.

For a delicious starter, try the fried green tomatoes. Save room for dessert—bourbon-laced pecan pie or fruit cobbler. Good California wine selection. Live jazz on Saturday nights.

Downtown

Georgia Brown's, 950 15th St. NW (on McPherson Square); (202) 393-4499. Monday-Thursday, 11:30 a.m.-11 p.m.; Friday, 11:30 a.m-midnight; Saturday, 5:30 p.m.-midnight; Sunday, 11:30 a.m.-4 p.m., 5:30-11 p.m. Metro Station: McPherson Square.

38 / Dance Clubs for 20- and 30-Somethings

The Spy Club and Zei

Entering the dance clubs listed here usually requires waiting in line. Some view this as a way to put the moves on new dancing partners.

Since its media-blitzed opening in 1991, The Spy Club has kept its best foot forward as a prime fun-preserve of the young upscale crowd. The chic decor incorporates gilt-edged paintings and little tables with twinkling candles. Intimate alcoves off the dance floor have comfortable seating and seductive candlelight. The Spy Club has firm notions about proper dress: No sneakers or t-shirts or jeans here. It's a place to strut a sexy step in the duds of your dreams (providing they're not nightmares). Eclectic music. Deejays. Cover.

Formerly an electric power station, Zei (pronounced Zee, Greek for life) has been adding new sparks to the stylish club scene since it opened in 1994. The techno-chic decor incorporates a wall more than forty feet high, with some forty video monitors constantly beaming down images. On a platform centered on the dance floor, a lone dancer shows off the latest moves. There's comfortable seating in alcoves at various levels, or you can hang out around the balcony rails. The third level is a private club and a great place to survey the action. Leave those sneakers and jeans at home and dress up for Zei. Disco music. Deejays. Cover. Zei and The Spy Club, just steps away from each other, attract a similar upscale crowd.

Downtown

The Spy Club, 805 15th St. NW (between H and I streets); (202) 289-1779. Wednesdays 5-10 p.m.; Thursdays until 2 a.m.; Fridays and Saturdays until 3 a.m. Happy hour on Fridays 5-9:30 p.m..

Zei, 1415 Zei Alley NW (between H and I streets); (202) 842-2445. Wednesday and Thursday 9 p.m.-2 a.m.; Friday and Saturday until 3 a.m. Metro Station: McPherson Square.

39 / Dance (etc.) Hangouts

The Insect Club, Planet Fred, and The Ritz

If there's an unidentified flying object in your soup at the Insect Club, don't complain to the waiter. It could be the chef's new specialty.

The Insect Club's decor and cuisine are true to its name. This tri-level nightspot, decked out with supersized insects and an ant farm, serves dishes such as puff pastry with crickets/mealworms topped with crumbled blue cheese and white dill sauce, or the insect du jour (ask your server). The club is also a hip spot for pizza, buffalo wings, and Jello shots, as well as dancing and pool. The dress code is "anything goes." Music is high-decibel rock. It's three blocks from those other bug experts, the FBI.

Futuristic decor; tri-level layout; young crowd. Planet Fred is under the same management as the Insect Club, but has a unique other-worldly look. No bugs, either.

Welcome to a world where music meets fashion: the Ritz. Five dance floors on four levels, each swing to a different deejay-driven beat. Choose reggae, top 40, rhythm and blues, or another sound, and dress to the nines. What you see at this club, which caters to upscale black professionals, are some of the latest fashion looks of the season on both disco-divas and their partners. Men must wear jackets. Live jazz Tuesday, Friday, and Saturday. Near the FBI building.

Downtown

The Insect Club, 625 E St. NW (between 6th and 7th streets); (202) 347-8884. Monday-Thursday, 4 p.m.-1:30 a.m.; Friday, 4 p.m.-3 a.m.; Saturday, 9 p.m.-3 a.m. Cover. Metro Station: Gallery Place-Chinatown.

Planet Fred, 1221 Connecticut Ave. NW; (202) 466-2336. Daily, 11 a.m.-2 a.m. Metro Station: Dupont Circle.

The Ritz, 919 E St. NW (between 9th and 10th streets); (202) 638-2582. Open Thursday and Friday, 5 p.m.-3 a.m.; Saturday, 9 p.m.-4 a.m.; Sunday, 9 p.m.-2 a.m. Cover. Metro Station: Metro Center or Gallery Place-Chinatown.

40 / Enjoy a Victorian B & B
The Reeds'

Splendid is the word for Jackie and Charles Reed's impeccably restored Victorian mansion set amid flower- and fountain-filled gardens. The Reeds' 1871 brownstone is a showcase for the exceptional collection of Victorian and art nouveau furnishings and appointments they have found over the years.

Everywhere you look in the house there is something of exquisite beauty. The parlor is hushed and elegant behind shuttered bay windows, with a turn-of-the-century player piano, a velvet settee and side chairs, rich rugs, and stained glass. The dining room boasts a gleaming antique banquet table, a working fireplace, and a breakfront full of old china and glassware.

A grand staircase leads to five bedrooms, each a gem with a different decor. Yours might have a wicker or canopied bed, a dainty writing table, a rocker, an ornate mantel, and a chintz-covered chaise. The rooms are stocked with books and magazines. They have telephones, color TVs, and air conditioning.

Breakfast—continental on weekdays and full on weekends—is served either in the dining room or on the Victorian-style porch.

Separate from the main house is an apartment accommodating five, with contemporary furniture, kitchen, and washer and dryer. There's no maid service in the apartment; you make your own bed and breakfast.

A family album shows the house when the Reeds acquired it in 1975. What they thought would take six months to shape up took eight years, ran way over budget, and turned their lives into a continuous version of television's This Old House.

The Reeds' adjoins historic Logan Circle; it's ten blocks from the White House.

Downtown

The Reeds', c/o Bed & Breakfast Accommodations, Ltd., P.O. Box 12011, Washington, D.C. 20005; (202) 328-3510. Metro Station: McPherson Square or Dupont Circle.

41 / Entertaining Kids

The Lively Arts

There's a wide variety of children's entertainment in D.C., much of it free. The cornucopia of fun includes puppet shows, plays, dancing, music, telling of stories (some to participate in and others to sit quietly throughout). Youngsters' activities are mainly on weekends and holidays, although some are more frequent. The *Washington Post*'s "Weekend" section is a good resource for special events that are in town for limited runs. Always check the museums and Kennedy Center for special kids' activities, too. Following are some choice children's selections:

See Show-Biz Acts Puppets, dancers, mimes, and singers perform just for kids in a historic theater. "Saturday Morning at the National," 1321 Pennsylvania Ave. NW; (202) 783-3372; October-April, reservations required. Metro Station: Metro Center.

Enjoy Live Theater, Puppet Shows, Storytelling Don't pass up these programs especially for preschoolers to eighth-graders. Discovery Theater, Arts and Industries Building, 900 Jefferson St. SW; (202) 357-1500. October-June. Metro Station: Smithsonian.

Giggle in a Museum Laugh out loud at the cartoons and children's films at the Hirshhorn Saturdays at 11 a.m. The Mall; Independence Avenue SW at 8th St.; (202) 357-2700. Metro Station: L'Enfant Plaza.

Thrill to a Military Band Concerts are presented June-August at 8 p.m. each Sunday, Tuesday, Thursday, and Friday. The Mall, Sylvan Theater, near Washington Monument; (202) 426-6841. Concerts also at the U.S. Capitol, west terrace at 8 p.m. each Tuesday, Wednesday, and Friday; (202) 619-7222. Metro Station: Smithsonian.

Shout Out Suggestions for Skits and See Them Acted Out "Now This!", an improvisational Saturday matinee cabaret act for kids, takes place in the Marquee Lounge at the Omni Shoreham Hotel, 2500 Calvert St. NW; (202) 745-1023. Metro Station: Woodley Park-Zoo.

42 / Fishing Trip for Small Fry

National Aquarium

By no means is the National Aquarium a "great" aquarium, but it merits a listing here as "great for tots." Think of it as their preface to a great aquarium.

For the ultimate in aquariums, visit nearby Baltimore's $21-million facility; it's a worthwhile excursion. By comparison, the National Aquarium is vest-pocket in size. It was state-of-the-art in its heyday, a day long past.

Founded in 1873 and operated today by the private, non-profit National Aquarium Society, this is the oldest public aquarium in the United States. Its intimacy makes it both attractive and welcoming to young children.

The aquarium's special "touch tank" contains conches, sea urchins, crabs, and other fishy folk that kids can pick up.

Try to arrive by 2 p.m. any day except Friday to watch the fish eat lunch. Mondays, Wednesdays, and Saturdays are meal times for several varieties of sharks; piranhas are fed on Tuesdays, Thursdays, and Sundays.

The aquarium is located in the basement of the Department of Commerce building, a gargantuan structure spanning an entire block. When it was built in 1932, the Department of Commerce building was the largest government office building in the world.

The building is at the base of the Federal Triangle, the huge conglomeration of government buildings erected between 1929 and 1938. (Before the buildings were constructed, government employees worked throughout the city in rental offices.) Even earlier, this was a sleazy neighborhood known as "Murder Bay," full of rooming houses, brothels, and saloons.

Downtown

National Aquarium, Department of Commerce Building, Pennsylvania Ave. NW at 14th St.; (202) 482-2825. Open daily except December 25; 9 a.m.-5 p.m. Adults $2; children 75 cents. Shop, cafeteria. Metro Station: Federal Triangle.

43 / Great Bargains

Tips for Budget Travelers

Bedtime Bargains Hotel rates are lowest on weekends, around holidays, mid-winter, and late summer. For free information on accommodations and other aspects of Washington, D.C., call or write (one month in advance) to: The Washington, D.C. Convention and Visitors Association, 1212 New York Ave. NW, #600, Washington, D.C. 20005-3992; (202) 789-7000.

Get the Where Is on the Whatchamacallit Here are top sources for free information on what to see and do in Washington, D.C.: The National Park Service (NPS) in East Potomac Park, near the Jefferson Memorial; and the new White House Visitors Center, Department of Commerce, 1450 Pennsylvania Ave. NW; (202) 208-1631, 1633. The *Washington Post*'s "Weekend" section is another good reference.

Use the Metro System A $5 one-day pass permits one person unlimited trips on Metrobus and Metrorail from 9:30 a.m. to midnight weekdays and all day weekends; (202) 637-7000.

Free Walks Walking tours are offered by the National Park Service, (202) 485-9880, and the Smithsonian's Resident Associate program, (202) 357-3030. *The Washington Street Map and Visitor Guide*, available free at Traveler's Aid in Union Station and at many hotels, includes self-guided walking tours; connect with Anthony Pitch's free Adams-Morgan tour (see page 74).

Cheap, Delicious Eats In Adams-Morgan, D.C.'s melting-pot neighborhood, you can munch your way almost around the world at ethnic restaurants where a meal runs under $10.

Wild Life Just a birdcall away from downtown D.C. are parks offering a wealth of free recreational activities, such as hiking and fitness trails, as well as opportunities for birding and nature study. Also, several historic gardens offer havens without charge. Call the District of Columbia Department of Recreation, (202) 673-7660.

44 / Off to a Great Start: Day 1, Part 2

Willard Inter-Continental

Enter the Willard Room and you will be transported back to the turn of the century, when opulent decor and lavish meals were the rage and the Willard opened in this distinctive marble beaux arts building. The Willard's thirty-dish breakfast buffet in fact outshines those old-time feasts by offering far more abundance, and it adds a strictly '90s twist, both for today's dieters and those with less restraint. (Offered Monday-Friday, 6:30-10:30 a.m.; $20.)

While the waiter pours fresh juices, you can check out the room, looking for famous pols. They gather here not only for the copious food, but also because the well-spaced tables provide privacy for important conversations. Then it's off to the buffet table for your selections. Among the offerings are berries, melons, and other fruits; muffins, bagels, croissants, and pastries, several flavored yogurts; and butter, cheeses, honey, and jams. The oak buffet holds the hot dishes—eggs and breakfast meats; it also has an array of dry cereals. The coffee could be stronger, but along with regular and herbal teas, it polishes off the meal. At lunch and dinner, the Willard Room serves pricey New American cuisine.

The Willard had greeted every president from Franklin Pierce to Dwight Eisenhower. But when the current building—dating from 1901—fell on hard times in 1968, it was closed. Renovators in 1984 found they had to start almost from scratch; the years of neglect had destroyed everything but the foundation.

Since then, the hotel's elaborate historic interiors have been faithfully reproduced, not only in the Willard Room but in other main public rooms. Guest rooms have period reproduction furnishings. Each also has a mini-bar and well-fitted bathroom. The sixth floor, designed with strict security measures, frequently houses visiting heads of state.

Downtown

Willard Inter-Continental, 1401 Pennsylvania Ave. NW (at 14th St.); (202) 628-9100; (800) 327-0200. Metro Station: Metro Center.

45 / Other Lincoln Memorials

Ford's Theater, Lincoln Museum, and Petersen House

The vacant rocking chair in the empty flag-draped box in Ford's Theater eerily recalls the night of April 14, 1865, when President Lincoln was assassinated by John Wilkes Booth while watching a performance of *Our American Cousin*. Booth crept into the box, fired his derringer, and escaped by jumping to the stage, mounting his horse in the back alley, and galloping away. He was captured and killed twelve days later on a farm in Virginia.

The theater, closed for more than one hundred years, was authentically restored in the 1960s. It is now maintained by the National Park Service.

The basement of Ford's Theater houses the Lincoln Museum. Exhibits include the clothes Lincoln was wearing when he was shot; Booth's pistol; Booth's diary, explaining his reasons for his actions; and other mementos.

Today, Ford's Theater is used for plays and pop concerts. There are daily tours except during rehearsals and Sunday and Thursday matinees (call ahead to check).

After Lincoln was wounded, he was carried across the street to the home of tailor William Petersen. Walk over to Petersen House to see the small back room where Lincoln was tended through the night by a twenty-three-year-old doctor, Charles Augustus Leale. While Lincoln's wife and son waited in the front room, Secretary of War Stanton met with his cabinet in an adjoining bedroom to begin the investigation of the assassination. Lincoln died the following morning in the Petersen house. The blood-stained pillowcases and pillow are authentic. Other Petersen House furnishings are period reproductions. *Downtown*

Ford's Theater and Lincoln Museum, 511 10th St. NW (between E and F streets); (202) 347-4833. Daily 9 a.m.-5 p.m.; Sunday 9 a.m.-2 p.m.; free; book shop.

Petersen House, 516 10th St. NW; (202) 426-6830. Daily 9 a.m-5 p.m.; free. Metro Station: Metro Center.

46 / Praising Women

National Museum of Women in the Arts

Up and down the Mall, you go in and out of monuments dedicated to famous men. Now to praise some famous women. . . .

The National Museum of Women in the Arts was founded in 1981 by Wilhelmina Cole Holladay and her husband, Wallace, with works from their own fabulous collection, which spans women's art from the Renaissance to the twentieth century. The museum opened in 1987 amid objections by some who believe that artists should not be segregated by gender.

The National Museum of Women in the Arts is now universally accepted as a remarkable achievement and a showcase for the achievements of women in a range of arts. The Wallaces conceived of this museum as a way of making up in part for the bias shown by most other museums, where men get disproportionate representation.

A renovated six-floor Renaissance Revival-style building (formerly headquarters of the all-male Masonic Grand Lodge) makes a grand setting for the artworks. Exhibits are drawn from the permanent collection of about fifteen hundred works by four hundred women, the majority from the Wallaces' holdings.

In the collection are works by well-known American impressionist Mary Cassatt and modernist Georgia O'Keeffe; more recent painters such as Helen Frankenthaler and Judy Chicago are also represented. But more exciting is discovering such works as the sixteenth-century portrait by Lavinia Fontana and those by Elisabeth Vigee LeBrun, court painter to Marie Antoinette. It's also a treat to see the work of early female silversmiths and Chinese nuns and artisans.

Downtown

National Museum of Women in the Arts, 1250 New York Ave. NW at 13th St.; (202) 783-5000. Monday-Saturday, 10 a.m.-5 p.m.; Sunday, noon-5 p.m. Closed Thanksgiving, December 25, January 1. $3 adults, $2 children. Café. Shop. Metro Station: Metro Center.

47 / Romancing the Past

Morrison-Clark Inn

Standing on the porch of the Morrison-Clark Inn, you can almost hear the rustle of starched petticoats as ladies of long ago strolled the grounds. Or is that a glimpse of Mamie's bangs or Jackie's pillbox hat in the pier glass?

Only one inn in the nation's capital is on the National Register of Historic Places, and this is it. It was built in 1864 as two separate three-story town houses for wealthy owners. The building's next owner added the graceful Chinese Chippendale porch and distinctive Shanghai mansard roof, transforming it into a Victorian/Chinoise fantasy, filled with treasures from the Orient.

In 1923, the Soldiers, Sailors, Marines, and Airmen's Club moved in. They maintained it for fifty-seven years as an inexpensive hotel for servicemen. First ladies were dedicated fund-raisers for the club, especially Mamie Eisenhower and Jacqueline Kennedy.

Today, guests enter the fifty-four-room inn through double glass doors and are treated to a rich re-creation of a Victorian parlor, complete with tufted upholstery and elegant flower arrangements. Complimentary continental breakfast is served in the adjoining Club Room with original marble fireplace.

Each guest room is uniquely and charmingly appointed with antiques or period reproductions. Some have private porches or fireplaces or bay windows; there might be a wooden bedstead or delicate wicker furniture. A bedspread in one room belonged to a former mistress of the mayor of old New York. Rooms have fresh flowers and updated bathrooms. Modern comforts such as cable TV are hidden in armoires. Furnishings are simpler in the new wing. The Morrison-Clark Inn's acclaimed restaurant (see page 50) serves New Southern food.

Downtown

Morrison-Clark Inn, 1015 L St. NW (between Massachusetts Avenue and 11th Street); (202) 898-1200; (800) 332-7898. On-site fitness room. Metro Station: Metro Center or Gallery Place-Chinatown.

48 / Superb New Southern Food

Morrison-Clark Restaurant

For several years, Chef Susan McCreight Lindeborg has been changing the way people think of Southern food by wedding it to techniques and ingredients from all over the world. The result has been deserved acclaim for her inventiveness and a bombardment of wonderful tastes for diners in a memorable setting.

A tiny, chic oasis in a National Historic Register inn with the intimate ambience of a Victorian salon, the Morrison-Clark Restaurant is white with handsome floor-to-ceiling mahogany-rimmed pier mirrors and matching Carrara marble fireplaces on the side walls. Small tables are accented with bright flowers, and a giant palm tops a round-centered settee rimmed with a few more tables. Sunlight floods the room at lunch; diners are bathed in soft candlelight at dinner. Waiters are well-informed about the menu as well as matching wines to foods.

First your server brings a dish of Tabasco-tinged pecans, perfect nibblers while you take in the room and look over the menu, which changes with both the seasons and the chef's desires.

Lindeborg's Southern muse believes in exotic intermarriages. Soft-shell crabs in ginger vinaigrette partner udon noodle pancakes and baby bok choy; curry-flour-dusted catfish are served with black-eyed pea cakes with aioli. Greens-stuffed rabbit loin gets a bourbon sauce; a creamy grits souffle (a signature dish) accompanies honey-roasted pork loin.

Appetizers might be Cajun dirty rice with duck liver and fried okra, or romaine-Roquefort salad with walnut focaccia. The lemon sponge roll—and all other desserts—are top-notch.

Downtown

Morrison-Clark Restaurant, 1015 L St. NW (between Massachusetts Ave. and 11th Street); (202) 898-1200. Lunch, Monday-Friday 11:30 a.m.-2 p.m. Dinner daily, 6-9 p.m. Brunch, Sunday 11:30 a.m.- 2 p.m. Reservations recommended. Metro Station: Metro Center or Gallery Place-Chinatown.

49 / Treasury of Documents
National Archives

Early in your visit, make an appointment for a fascinating in-depth tour of the National Archives, the repository of our nation's most hallowed documents; (202) 501-5205.

Or, join the line of people waiting to see the original Declaration of Independence, U.S. Constitution, and Bill of Rights at John Russell Pope's white marble neoclassic building.

At precisely 10 a.m., two huge bronze doors slide ceremoniously open, bringing these esteemed documents into view in the rotunda within protective glass and bronze cases.

Notice the dent in one of the bronze cases? It's a reminder that in 1986 someone tried to break the glass and destroy our Bill of Rights. Each night the documents are lowered twenty feet into a fifty-ton vault that protects them from theft, the elements, and destruction by nuclear blast.

In the side cases are rotating exhibits; on permanent display in the rotunda is one of the four existing copies of the 1297 version of the Magna Carta, one of the documents ensuring basic English rights and privileges. (Its owner is billionaire politician/maverick Ross Perot.) The Circular Gallery houses additional exhibits.

The National Archives is not just a museum. It houses billions of papers and collateral materials from American history, ranging from the Emancipation Proclamation to the far-out portrait of President Nixon painted on a grain of rice. It's a renowned facility for checking genealogical records. Alex Haley began researching *Roots* here. The archives' resources are available to those sixteen or older with a valid photo I.D. (Information in Room 404; Pennsylvania Avenue entrance.)

Downtown

National Archives, Constitution Ave. NW, between 7th and 9th streets; information (202) 501-5000; research (202) 501-5400. Daily 10 a.m.-5 p.m.; April 1-Labor Day, to 9 p.m.; free. Shop. Metro Station: Archives-Navy Memorial.

50 / Trendy New Italian

Notte Luna

If you want to stoke up on the carbs before or after dancing at The Spy Club or Zei, your goal is nearby Notte Luna, where pastas are anything but ordinary and the decor is almost Felliniesque. Even the rest rooms are a trip: Italian language tapes broadcast over the PA system. Notte Luna is a fine place to explore New Italian food—Italian cuisine that has detoured into California.

This glamorous spot combines neon strips with the buttresses on the high churchlike ceiling. Black marble accents the sunburst lighting, tromp l'oeil murals, an open kitchen, wood-burning pizza oven, and decidedly upscale clientele. Portions are generous and waiters knowledgeable and friendly.

Working on those portfolios can make a person hungry, so young professionals dig in to the complimentary cheese focaccia while consulting the menu and well-edited wine list. The menu changes from time to time, but follows themes similar to those in this write-up.

Notte Luna is known for its brick-oven pizza with cracker-thin crust; for starters or a late-night snack, you might try the classic quattro formaggio (four cheeses) or pizza with an antipasto topping. For a lighter start, there's smoked salmon carpaccio or a lively Caesar salad.

Typically, the pastas might include orecchiette with pesto-roasted mushrooms and pomodoro sauce, or rigatoni with spicy veal ragú and cured olives. Interesting main courses might be pesto-stuffed chicken breast with pine-nut romano cheese crust and sun-dried tomatoes, or something simpler such as grilled strip steak or braised lamb shank.

Downtown

Notte Luna, 809 15th St. NW (between H and I streets); (202) 408-9500. Monday-Thursday, 11 a.m.-11 p.m.; Friday, 11 a.m.-midnight; Saturday, 5 p.m.-midnight; Sunday, 5-11 p.m. Reservations recommended. Metro Station: McPherson Square.

51 / Tip-Top Tudor Treat
Henley Park Hotel

Imagine an English country house where there's proper tea in the afternoon. "So, what's this got do with Washington, D.C.?" you say. Answer: It's the description of the Henley Park Hotel.

Built in 1918 as an apartment house in typical Tudor style, the Henley Park is encrusted with leaded glass and 120 gargoyles and plaques. Can you guess which gargoyles are the owners' faces? (Hint: Look for a cigar.) Meticulously restored as a ninety-six-room hotel in 1982, the Henley Park is named for a picturesque little town on the Thames. An imaginative blend of traditional furnishings creates a country-house atmosphere.

On the ground floor, the Wilkes Room combines Oriental rugs with fresh flowers, comfortable armchairs, and a commanding fireplace. Afternoon tea is served here. And what a tea it is: tiny scones, dainty smoked salmon sandwiches, biscuits ("veddy" proper English cookies), bowls of clotted cream, and an array of teas.

Marley's Lounge, also on the ground floor, has mauve-tinted leaded-glass windows that cast a sexy glow over the surroundings, chairs upholstered in tapestry, and a dark-wood bar at one end. On weekends, live jazz makes this intimate space seem like a private club. The hotel's highly regarded Coeur de Léon restaurant is covered separately in this guide (see page 54).

Guest rooms convey country-house coziness, with colorful chintz spreads and drapes, print upholstered chairs, and mahogany eighteenth-century reproductions. Well-appointed bathrooms have custom-designed mosaic-tiled floors.

Fitness facilities are one block away. You're walking distance from the National Portrait Gallery, National Museum of American Art, and Chinatown. A limousine services downtown and Capitol Hill.

Downtown

Henley Park Hotel, 926 Massachusetts Ave. NW; (202) 638-5200, (800) 222-8474. Metro Station: Metro Center or Gallery Place-Chinatown.

52 / Wine and Dine Royally

Coeur de Léon

At one time, hotel restaurants took a bum rap. Now, with top chefs, some are desirable D.C. dining destinations—such as Coeur de Léon in the Henley Park Hotel. Under the direction of executive chef Jon Dornbusch, Coeur de Léon's kitchen turns out distinctive and creative New American Continental cuisine. Dornbusch combines the freshest possible ingredients in unusual combinations, with a hint of classicism in pretty presentations.

Named for the crest of Richard the Lion-Hearted (an English king) over the entry archway, Coeur de Léon offers two settings— a romantic glassed-in atrium with exposed brick walls, soft lighting, and bountiful greenery, and a hushed bi-level dining room with mirror-covered pillars, stained-glass windows, and a soothing mauve-and-taupe color scheme. Guests wear casual or dressy apparel, and the service is friendly but professional.

Sip a glass of bubbly while studying the menu and the well-conceived wine list. Fish and seafood are popular here; meat and poultry also are well prepared. Start with an exotic creation such as grilled shrimp with frizzled leeks and citrus emulsion, or something lighter, such as a fresh and pungent field-green salad, or meaty portabello mushrooms with basil purée and green olive tapenade. Main courses might include grouper with lemon-thyme capellini and grilled zucchini; lump crab cakes in a pool of roasted tomato coulis; or crispy vegetable strudel with mesculin greens, a special dish for the dieter.

Desserts feature updates of homey recipes such as bread pudding, as well as tarts and sorbets. You might also treat yourself to Barsac, a lemony-sweet French dessert wine.

Downtown

Coeur de Léon, 926 Massachusetts Ave. NW (in the Henley Park Hotel); (202) 638-5200. Lunch 11:30 a.m.-2:30 p.m.; dinner 6-10 p.m.; Sunday brunch 11:30 a.m.-2:30 p.m.; tea 4-6 p.m. Reservations recommended. Metro Station: Metro Center or Gallery Place-Chinatown.

53 / Seeing the White House

White House Tour

Seeing America's greatest house means also seeing a great cross-section of Americans.

"Did Jackie do that?" the woman in the jogging suit asks her similarly attired friend as they see a piano in the Entrance Hall. The two friends are in line with hundreds of other people, trying to see the White House on a regular tour. They have inched their way past the guards with Mountie-style hats and listened to the commentary from PA speakers hidden in the bushes.

The women ponder the "Jackie decor" question as they begin the tour. Five of the 132 rooms in the mansion are open to the public. The women start with the East Room, with its Gilbert Stuart portrait of George Washington that Dolley Madison saved when the British set fire to the building; then they tour the Green Room (named for its green silk walls), once Thomas Jefferson's dining room.

They are rewarded in the Blue Room: The guard explains that when Mrs. John F. Kennedy learned that the walls of this room were white during the Madison administration, she had them covered in white silk. Pat Nixon had them redone in the current blue-trimmed beige paper. Still to come are the Red Room and the huge State Dining Room.

The White House was designed by Irish architect James Hoban, who was inspired by Ireland's mansions.

Downtown

White House Tour, 1600 Pennsylvania Ave. NW; tours (202) 456-7041. Open Tuesday-Saturday, 10 a.m.-noon; free. If you don't have a VIP pass (see page 1), join the line at the White House Visitor Center (8 a.m.-5 p.m.; Memorial Day to Labor Day, 7 a.m.-7 p.m.), Department of Commerce Bldg., 1450 Pennsylvania Avenue NW; (Metro Station: Metro Center) for tickets required from March 2 to September 2 (no tickets required mid-Sept. to mid-March). Lines form as early as 6:30 a.m. for tickets. There's a limit of six per person. No tours during State visits and various other times. Metro Stop: McPherson Square, Federal Triangle.

54 / Wonderful View
Old Post Office Observatory

Washingtonians love to do architectural CPR on their buildings, breathing life and health into property slated for the wrecker's ball (see Union Station, page 12). Thanks to this proclivity, the Old Post Office, a Romanesque Revival building completed in 1899, has become a first-class tourist attraction, with shops, cafés, free live entertainment in the afternoons, and a fabulous view.

The Old Post Office was slated for demolition in the 1920s because its fanciful silhouette did not conform to the sleek plans for the Federal Triangle. Lack of money during the Depression gave the building a reprieve until the preservationists saved it forever.

Renovation started in 1978, and the Old Post Office Pavilion opened in 1984. It featured kiosks selling assorted knick-knacks, restaurants, and cafés serving ethnic foods. More shops, restaurants, a bar, and a miniature golf course were added to the three-story glass-enclosed atrium in 1992.

The building's 315-foot-high tower—once considered an eyesore—is now a handsome observation deck with extra-spacious windows. It will be the highlight of your visit here. Free tower tours leave every five to seven minutes. The glass-fronted elevator whisks you to the ninth floor in forty-seven seconds! Another elevator takes you to the twelfth-floor observation deck. You'll feel you are up much higher than that.

Be sure to walk down one flight to see the ten Congress bells. They were cast at the same foundry that made Westminster Abbey's bells and they are rung when Congress opens and closes and on federal holidays.

Downtown

Old Post Office Observatory, Pennsylvania Ave. and 12th St. NW; (202) 289-4224. Tower open March-September daily 9 a.m.-11 p.m.; October-February daily 10 a.m.-6 p.m.; free. Metro Station: Federal Triangle.

55 / Make It a Dim Sum Sunday

Chinatown and Beyond

In the shadow of the colorful seventy-five-foot-wide Friendship Arch across 7th and H streets, testifying to the sister-city tie between Beijing and Washington, D.C., is minuscule Chinatown. The Arch is between G, E, 5th, and 8th streets; Metro Station: Gallery Place-Chinatown.

Don't be put off by the run-down neighborhood or careworn restaurants. These no-frills places offer an array of tasty fare from several regions—from mild Cantonese to hot and spicy Hunan and Szechuan—and stray into Burma (Myanmar), too.

The traditional dim sum tea lunch of savory dishes is especially pleasant on a Sunday afternoon, though it's served seven days a week at lunch. A moveable buffet, dim sum permits tasting many different dishes. Waiters wheel around snack-laden carts for your perusal; dumplings are a good first choice. At the end of the meal, your plates are tallied for your bill ($1-$4 per plate).

Some of the tastiest dim sum are served in two Chinatown restaurants. Don't miss the China Inn, 631 H St. NW, between 6th and 7th streets; (202) 842-0909, and Mr. Yung's Restaurant, 740 6th St. NW, between G and H streets; (202) 628-1098. Both open for lunch and dinner; dim sum is served 1-3 p.m. Both restaurants also offer a variety of Cantonese dishes. Metro Station for both: Gallery Place-Chinatown.

To mix people-watching with your Peking duck, go to City Lights of China in the Dupont Circle area, where D.C. insiders eat regularly; 1730 Connecticut Ave. NW, between R and S streets; (202) 265-6688; Weekdays, lunch and dinner; dinner only Saturday and Sunday. Reservations recommended. Metro Station: Dupont Circle. Choose from Mandarin, Cantonese, and Szechuan dishes in many inventive combinations. Try anything on the menu here; you won't be disappointed. The pleasant, tiered dining room is comfortable with banquettes and booths.

Chinatown

56 / Authors' and Gourmets' Gathering Place

Radisson Barceló Hotel

The Radisson Barceló Hotel boasts of some of the largest guest rooms in D.C. and some of the most widely known guests. The hotel's "Author's Suite" resembles a TV-talk-show set for media wishing to interview such diverse celebrities as Desmond Tutu and Cybill Shepherd. A sunbelt tour awaits your tastebuds in the hotel's bright hacienda-like, highly praised Gabriel restaurant.

Acquired in 1992 by the Barceló Group, a family-owned travel company in Mallorca, Spain, the hotel officially reopened in 1994 after extensive renovations. Typical rooms are decorated in soothing subtle neutrals and dark woods. The swimming pool on the second floor overlooks a delightful courtyard.

Comfortable and casual, the restaurant Gabriel (named for the hotel's owner) has stucco walls, bright colors, and dark woods. Award-winning chef Greggory Hill offers a fresh view of cuisines from the American Southwest, Mediterranean, Spain, and Mexico. The wine list features selections from Spain and California. Some main dishes are available in both small and large portions.

For those interested in trying a little bit of a lot of things, there are tapas with a wide range of sherry to sip with them. A chewy, crusty bread, served with garlic-rosemary olive oil for dipping, keeps you munching until your meal arrives. Starters always include smoked black bean soup with shredded chicken, and jicama slaw with cumin-flavored chips. Among the main dishes might be skewered monkfish served with sautéed spinach dressed with pine nuts, raisins, and olive oil; a moist and tender rosemary-parsley-thyme rotisserie chicken; or seasonal game-and-fig stew. For dessert, try the Mexican chocolate ice cream or the fruit-filled phyllo with custard and apricot coulis. *Dupont Circle*

Radisson Barceló Hotel, 2121 P St. NW (between 21st and 22nd streets); (202) 293-3100, (800) 333-3333. Metro Station: Dupont Circle.

57 / Beautiful Threads

The Textile Museum

In this wash-and-wear era, you can still admire and study an astonishing range of the world's finest, rarest, and most historic handmade textiles—at the Textile Museum.

The collection was started by George Hewitt Myers (1875-1957), an heir to the Bristol Myers fortune, when he bought an Oriental rug for his dorm room at Yale. Myers's passion for textiles and rugs culminated in this museum, whose holdings include fifth-century Coptic textiles, Kashmiri embroideries, pre-Columbian tapestries, and twentieth-century textiles from Central and South America and the American Southwest.

The collection is housed in two elegant turn-of-the-century buildings that were converted into a museum in 1925. The building serving as the museum entrance, shop, and administrative offices, originally Myers's home, was designed by John Russell Pope, architect of the Jefferson Memorial and the west wing of the National Gallery of Art. The adjoining building, designed by Waddy B. Wood, houses exhibition galleries and the thirteen-thousand-volume Arthur D. Jenkins Library.

Rotating exhibits display works from the vast museum collection. Special exhibits might borrow from private collections to show textiles from the remote corners of the world, or present the works of contemporary fiber artists.

Textiles and rugs have long been appreciated for their beauty and utility, but their role in world history and culture is rarely explored. This knowledge gap is filled by the exhibits, symposia, and events at the Textile Museum. In June, try to attend the museum's "Celebration of Textiles," a lighthearted romp with sheep-shearing, folk music, and other fun.

Dupont Circle

The Textile Museum, 2320 S St. NW (between 23rd and 24th streets); (202) 667-0441. Open Monday-Saturday 10 a.m.-5 p.m.; Sunday 1-5 p.m. Suggested donation: $5. Shop. Metro Station: Dupont Circle.

58 / Country Inn Near the Metro
Tabard Inn Hotel

The small, friendly, and informal Tabard Inn dates from World War I, when three stately Victorian town houses were linked together. Efforts to tear down the structures in the 1970s were defeated, and the Tabard Inn is now Washington's oldest hotel in continuous operation (a claim also made by Hotel Washington, opened in 1918). The Tabard Inn is named for a famous hostelry in Chaucer's *Canterbury Tales*. The establishment lives up to its slogan, "a country inn in the heart of the city."

If you like a slightly careworn, old-fashioned genteel ambience—and many do; the Tabard is enormously popular—this is a charming place to stay. If sleek decor and star-spangled service are more your thing, look elsewhere.

The forty rooms (twenty-five with private baths) vary greatly in size, shape, proportions, and decor. They are furnished with Victorian and American antiques that show their age. Some rooms are so atmospheric and beautifully appointed with period pieces that they might serve as a Merchant-Ivory movie set. One room has an upright piano. Several rooms have fireplaces. Some of the impressive bathrooms feature big claw-foot tubs.

Other rooms—perhaps former servants' quarters—are small and functional. Their lack of lavishness is reflected in their lower rates. All rooms have telephones, but no TV. Comfortable, homey lounges are scattered around the main floor.

The rates include continental breakfast. There is no room service, but you wouldn't have any at home, either. The hotel's highly regarded restaurant has a separate listing in this book (see page 61).

Dupont Circle

Tabard Inn Hotel, 1739 N St. NW (between 17th and 18th streets); (202) 785-1277. Reserve far in advance. Metro Station: Dupont Circle or Farragut North.

59 / Country Inn Dining

Tabard Inn Restaurant

A little inn in the country without the long drive and traffic jams: That's the feeling the Tabard Inn Hotel and its restaurant impart.

Near Dupont Circle on a quiet tree-lined street, the three cozy dining areas make a perfect retreat. You can eat on the main floor, upstairs overlooking the courtyard, or in the courtyard itself.

The Tabard Inn is well known for healthful New American cuisine. The Tabard grows its own produce without pesticides at its farm in Virginia; the meat is additive-free. Menus here rate high for quality, quantity, and originality. Since they are seasonally driven, they change often.

The specialties menu lists the week's harvest from the Tabard's farm; recently, it featured about twenty items, including six kinds of squash, several cabbages, pumpkins, turnips, and beets.

If you're bopping around the museums in and about Dupont Circle on a Saturday, take a Tabard brunch break (11 a.m.-2:30 p.m.). You'll find the farm greens decked out in a sherry vinaigrette dressing. Or, how about farm trout salad on homemade sourdough toast? Tabard dresses eggs lavishly: with spicy chicken sausages smothered in Muenster cheese.

At lunch or dinner you might try giant ravioli stuffed with sautéed exotic mushrooms and cheeses with basil puree, or luscious pecan-crusted chicken breast atop wilted greens with squash cornbread.

If you never eat sweets, break the rule here: The desserts are great. The best finale perhaps is a flourless chocolate cake served with maple-walnut and vanilla ice cream.

The Tabard Inn Restaurant has a nice selection of wine specials by the glass.

Weather permitting, eat in the courtyard; you'll feel countrified.

Dupont Circle

Tabard Inn Restaurant, 1739 N St. NW (between 17th and 18th streets); (202) 785-1277. Metro Station: Dupont Circle or Farragut North.

60 / Dine in a Mediterranean Hideaway

BeDuCi

From Monday through Friday at BeDuCi there's wonderful food and something else—a great bargain! The prix fixe lunch costs $11.95 at this cozy fifty-seat Mediterranean-style restaurant, where à la carte entrées top off at $24. BeDuCi—D.C. lingo for "BElow DUpont CIrcle"—has whitewashed walls and a happy atmosphere fostered by friendly owners Michelle Miller and Jean-Claude Garrat. The prix fixe lunch is continental cuisine. You'll want to return for a Mediterranean meal.

The bargain lunch menu changes every Monday and includes an appetizer such as bruschetta (toasted bread topped with cheese or tomatoes); salad or soup; a choice of fresh and flavorful pasta, chicken, or fish entrées; and coffee or tea. Dessert is extra—mainly in the $5.50-$6 range—and worth both the cash put out and calories taken in. Some of the best desserts are made by Ms. Miller. Two (or more) sweets lovers might try the sampler of her tiramisu, chocolate indulgence, and Frangelico cakes for $9.95.

Moroccan Chef Larbi's à la carte menu stars BeDuCi's Mediterranean specialties. Try his special rabbit in a tangy mustard sauce with fettucine, or grilled rockfish in a similar sauce; spinach with black-pepper noodles and duck breast; or mashed potatoes and muerguez (sausage). For vegetarians, there's an interesting Algerian couscous.

The huge international wine list displays Mr. Garrat's eclectic tastes. Appropriately, there are Mediterranean selections. The French wines include some of the finest vintage years. American wines range from California's offerings to lesser-known selections from Maryland, Virginia, Washington, and Oregon.

Dupont Circle

BeDuCi, 2014 P St. NW; (202) 467-4466. Lunch Monday-Friday 11:30 a.m.-2:30 p.m.; dinner Monday-Thursday 5:30-10 p.m., Friday-Saturday 5:30-10:30 p.m.; Sunday 5-10 p.m. Reservations recommended. Metro Station: Dupont Circle.

61 / Explore Small Cultural Treasuries

Dupont-Kalorama

Culture comes pleasantly in mansions turned into intimate museums, tucked between embassies and better-known museums in the Dupont-Kalorama area. Pick up a Dupont-Kalorama museum map at any of the museums; highlights are listed below.

Anderson House/Society of the Cincinnati This was home to Larz Anderson, minister to Belgium and ambassador to Japan, and his wife, Isabel Weld Perkins, whose passion for collecting is seen in the East-West appointments throughout the house. Anderson bequeathed the house and its contents to the Society of the Cincinnati, in which he was a member, for its headquarters. Founded in 1783, it is the oldest patriotic society in America.

The Historical Society of D.C./Heurich Mansion This splendor once belonged to a wealthy brewer, Christian Heurich, who built his mansion from 1892 to 1894 and lived in it until he died at age 102. Take a sack lunch and eat in the Victorian garden Tuesday-Friday, 10:30 a.m. to 5 p.m.

National Museum of American Jewish Military History The museum's compelling photographic exhibits cover Jewish participation in all wars, including the most recent. Archives contain valuable documents, among them minutes of the founders' meeting in 1896. Visitors can view extensive, relevant military memorabilia in the permanent exhibition.

Anderson House/Society of the Cincinnati, 2118 Massachusetts Ave. NW, between 21st and 22nd streets; (202) 785-2040. Tuesday-Saturday 1-4 p.m.; free. Concerts, lectures, special events.

The Historical Society of Washington, D.C./Heurich Mansion, 1307 New Hampshire Ave. NW; (202) 785-2068; Wednesday-Saturday noon-4 p.m. Garden free; $3 admission to house.

National Museum of American Jewish Military History, 1811 R St. NW (near New Hampshire Ave.); (202) 265-6280; Monday-Friday 9 a.m.-5:00 p.m. Sun 1-5 p.m.; closed official and Jewish holidays; free. Metro Station: Dupont Circle

62 / Gay D.C.

Bars, Clubs, and Church

Gay life in D.C. is centered around Dupont Circle and some clubs in the southeast. To get the latest details, pick up a copy of *The Washington Blade* at Lambda Rising (1625 Connecticut Ave. NW) or other neighborhood bookstores. The Gay and Lesbian Switchboard number is (202) 628-4667; special lesbian number, (202) 628-4666. Following are a few ideas to get you going.

In the Dupont Circle area, P Street is home to both the oldest gay bar in the neighborhood, Mr. P's—and one of the newest—Escándolo! Mr. P's, 2147 P St. NW; (202) 293-1064; Monday-Thursday 3 p.m.-2 a.m., Friday and Saturday, 3 p.m.-3 a.m., Sunday noon-2 a.m., has an established older clientele. Escándolo!, 2122 P St. NW; (202) 822-8909; Monday-Thursday 11 p.m.-2 a.m., Friday 11 a.m.-3 a.m., Saturday 4 p.m.-3 a.m., Sunday 4 p.m.-2 a.m., features young Latinos plus drag and dance shows. Metro Station for both: Dupont Circle.

In southeast D.C., Tracks is famous as a gay dance club that also attracts straights to its mammoth dance floor and superb deejay music, 1111 First St. SE; (202) 488-3320; Tuesday 9 p.m.-2 a.m., Wednesday, Thursday, and Sunday until 4 a.m., Friday and Saturday until 6 a.m. Cover. Metro Station: Eastern Market.

On a more serious side, make sure to see the Metropolitan Community Church, a masterpiece in modern ecclesiastical architecture by Suzanne Retig, in northwest Shaw. Shaped by the non-denominational congregation's convictions, the architectural message of Retig's two-story glass structure is a belief in being visibly who and what you are. Serving mainly gays and lesbians, the church provides solace in the age of AIDS; upstairs a chapel with special funerary urn niches form a columbarium, 475 Ridge St. NW; (202) 638-7373; services Sunday at 9 and 11 a.m. and 7 p.m., Wednesday at 6 p.m.; open 9 a.m.-5 p.m.; buzz for entry. Metro Station: Mount Vernon Square.

63 / Hop on the Brew Bandwagon

Survey of Beer Havens

Following are some tips on tapping into the trendy brew scene.

Beer-lovers find complete happiness at the pub-like Brickskeller, with more than five hundred different beers from everywhere in every conceivable style, from Aussie ales to U.S. micro-brewed stouts. Would-be connoisseurs can attend bimonthly beer tastings here. Bartenders open cans from the bottom for collectors, 1523 22nd St. NW, between P and Q streets; (202) 293-1885; Monday-Thursday 11:30 p.m.-2 a.m., Friday 11:30 a.m.-3 a.m., Saturday 6 p.m.-3 a.m., Sunday 6 p.m.-2 a.m. Metro Station: Dupont Circle.

The Saloon, a jazz-happy beer-lovers' Generation X hangout in Georgetown, has seventy-five different beers (eighteen on tap) plus budget steaks and burgers, 3239 M St. NW, near Potomac St.; (202) 338-4900; Sunday-Thursday 5 p.m.-2 a.m., Friday and Saturday 5 p.m.-3 a.m. Cover. Cheapies before 7 p.m. No nearby Metro Station.

Washington, D.C.'s only micro-brewery, Capitol City Brewing Company, has a handsome copper bar and metal stairway to the brew tanks, where beer is actually made. The decor weds old warehouse to roadside diner. The beers change daily; the big bulletin board lists selections—usually ales, a porter, stout, and lager. If you're feeling experimental, order a sampler. The menu is a good match with the brews—featuring sausages, pork chops, and burgers among the selections. This is a singles hot spot, and is jammed right after work. Near the Convention Center. Best time to eat here is early or late, 1100 New York Ave. NW; entrance, 11th and H streets; (202) 628-2222; lunch and dinner daily, 11:30 a.m.-midnight. Metro Station: Metro Center.

Hard Times Café has funky, homey ambience with great Southwest and Western micro-brews and Tex-Mex vittles, 1404 King St., Alexandria, Va.; (703) 683-5340; lunch and dinner daily; Metro Station: King St.

64 / Modern Art in Millionaire's Home

The Phillips Collection

When it opened to the public in 1921, the Phillips Collection became the first permanent museum for modern art in America. The collection is still housed in part in its original nineteenth-century building, which until 1931 was home to its founder, Duncan Phillips, a Pittsburgh millionaire. The twentieth-century Goh Annex also houses a portion of the collection.

Thanks to careful restoration and discreet modernization, the main museum retains the unpretentious private-home ambience Phillips felt was best for experiencing works of art. The paintings are installed as he wished—in "exhibition units" that show the artists in all their power. Visitors can stroll the well-proportioned rooms or relax in a comfortable chair to contemplate a fascinating work before moving on to the next masterpiece.

There are no uniformed guards here; instead, the Phillips employs art students and artists to answer visitors' questions.

One of the few Americans of his era to enthusiastically collect modern art (Solomon Guggenheim was another), Phillips began with American Impressionists and continued to buy whatever pleased his eclectic eye. He often backed lesser-known artists.

Among the approximately 2,500 works that currently make up the Phillips Collection are the largest American museum collection of Bonnard paintings (sixteen in all), as well as notable works by Goya, El Greco, Delacroix, Van Gogh, Degas, Monet, Renoir, Braque, Picasso, and Klee. The Americans include O'Keeffe, Marin, Rothko, and Pollack. Recent gifts are works by Diebenkorn and Picasso.

Dupont Circle

Phillips Collection, 1600–1612 21st St. NW (at Q St.); (202) 387-2151. Suggested contributions $6.50 adults and $3.25 students and seniors. Monday-Saturday 10 a.m.-5 p.m., Thursdays till 8:30 p.m., Sundays noon-7 p.m. Café and shop. Metro Station: Dupont Circle.

65 / Nibble, Mingle, and Schmooze
Survey of Café Bookstores

Tired of monument-hopping or strolling around town? Take a book-and-coffee break at these intriguing hangouts.

Kramerbooks & afterwords For many Washingtonians, Kramerbooks is the quintessential bookstore and café, with high-quality books and well-read employees to schmooze about them with customers. Coffee, snacks and meals; known singles meeting-place, 1517 Connecticut Ave. NW; (202) 387-1400. Metro Station: Dupont Circle.

Borders Books and Music This gargantuan chain store has a surprisingly local ambience. There's a no-frills café, but what makes Borders special is the lineup of in-store events ranging from country music workshops to conversations with filmmakers, 1801 K St. NW; (202) 466-4999. Metro Station: Farragut West or Farragut North.

Politics & Prose This café and bookstore is a favorite among artists, writers, and UDC students. The store takes a special interest in local writers' works, and throws great book-signing parties, 5015 Connecticut Ave. NW, between Nebraska Ave. and Fessenden St.; (202) 364-1919. Metro Station: Van Ness-UDC, then walk north.

Café Luna/Luna Books Café Luna serves Italian dishes indoors and outdoors. Luna books (housed in the same space) is where activists meet to eat dessert, buy books, and (of course) talk, 1633 P St. NW; bookstore, (202) 332-2543; café, (202) 387-4005. Metro Station: Dupont Circle.

Sidney Kramer Books There's no café at this fascinating store, but it offers a feast of VIPs. The store specializes in books that put D.C. under a microscope—politics, economics, defense, and business. Keep your eyes peeled for the many well-known politicians, ambassadors, military bigwigs, and Hill staffers who browse the shelves, 1825 I St. NW; (202) 293-2685. Metro Station: Farragut West.

66 / Experience a 1920s Time Capsule

Woodrow Wilson House Museum

Infinitely more intimate than you might expect of a former presidential residence, Woodrow Wilson House is, as the brochure says, a "unique time capsule history of the 1920s."

The twenty-eighth U.S. president was the only former president to stay on in Washington, D.C. after he left office. Wilson lived here from 1921 until his death in 1924. Wilson's second wife, Edith, stayed in this house until her death in 1961.

The red-brick Georgian Revival town house was designed by Waddy B. Wood, who also designed the Department of the Interior buildings and the National Museum of Women in the Arts. The house has been preserved as it was when the Wilsons occupied it, from the well-stocked kitchen to the sheet music for "Oh, You Beautiful Doll"—a favorite of Wilson's—on the grand piano in the parlor. To some tourists, intimacies such as these will be highlights of their visit.

Others will respond to the worldly memorabilia. Wilson, a former scholar, educator, and author, expanded the United States' leadership in world affairs. On view are mementos relating to the League of Nations, including the flag he had hoped would become the organization's emblem.

Wilson suffered a stroke near the end of his second term in office, and his wife saw to it that the house accommodated his needs. Upstairs is the huge Lincoln-size bed Mrs. Wilson had built, a copy of the one Wilson slept in at the White House. There is also an elevator, installed so the president could move from floor to floor more easily.

Dupont Circle

Woodrow Wilson House Museum, 2340 S St. NW (next to the Textile Museum); (202) 387-4062. Guided tours. Tuesday-Sunday 10 a.m.-4 p.m. Admission: $4 for adults, $2.50 for children. Metro Station: Dupont Circle, then seven blocks northwest on Massachusetts Ave.

67 / People Watch in Plush Surroundings

Washington's Hilton Hotels

Both Hiltons are prized for people-watching, as well as their as luxurious amenities. Even if you don't check-in you can check-out the action from comfortable lobby lounges, your hand wrapped around a drink.

The 1,123-room Washington Hilton and Towers, on Connecticut Avenue, draws conventioneers from all over the world, themselves, a colorful pageant, but you might also catch glimpses of famous pols parading by to grace head tables; or see some box-office star lending support to a cause. Meanwhile, the 549-room Capital Hilton downtown is prime territory for seeing lobbyists and other hot-shots with business on The Hill.

The hotels have distinctive personalities, each enchanced by recent renovations. The wing-shaped Washington Hilton and Towers is traditional/contemporary; its lobby is accented with mahogany millwork and furnished with cushy settees and chairs. At the Capital Hilton, the decor is neo-art deco, with milled cherrywood columns, sleek torchères and graceful staircases.

The hotels' rooms (WHT earth toned; CH jade and rust) feature oversized beds, refreshment centers, TVs with cable and movies, and marble bathrooms. Their Towers offer plusher VIP amenities including their own lounges and concierges. Both hotels have restaurants and shops, and workout rooms.

The Washington Hilton and Towers 1919 Grill has a Victorian aura, and serves praiseworthy seafood and steaks. Behind the hotel are tennis courts, a swimming pool, and café. Capital Hilton is walking distance from Official D.C.

Washington Hilton and Towers, 1919 Connecticut Avenue, (between Columbia Rd. & 19 St.); (202)-483-3000. Metro Station: Dupont Circle.

Capital Hilton, 1001 16th St. NW, (between K & L sts.); (202)-333-1000; Toll free for both hotels: 800-HILTONS. Metro Station: Farragut North & Farragut West.

68 / Small Seafood Café

Pesce

Two of Washington's most celebrated chefs, Roberto Donna (Galileo) and Jean-Louis Palladin (Jean-Louis), are owners of Pesce, a small retail fish market and thirty-five-seat café, with the bright and cheerful ambience of a good restaurant in a small Mediterranean seaport. The opening of bistros and cafés by chefs of high-priced restaurants is a D.C. trend. That two rival chefs teamed up in such a venture surprised many restaurant-goers.

Since the fish served at Pesce is bought daily, specials are listed on blackboard menus. In the market section, fresh fish are displayed in a glass case like works of art. Pasta dishes and excellent focaccia also appear on the menu.

A meal for two might consist of prawns with stuffed squash and a risotto, with lobster in truffle sauce. Other unusual offerings might be shrimp tempura served over red-pepper sauce, and halibut in black-olive butter. For the less adventurous, there is always broiled fish or mussels steamed in wine and shallots.

Despite its illustrious owners, Pesce is a casual, neighborhood café with such a subtle sign that you might just stroll right by it. Pesce is situated in an area made for meandering after your meal. Watch for marvelous old mansions that are now embassies or museums (see the Textile Museum, page 59, the Heurich Mansion, page 63, and the Phillips Collection, page 66). Or stroll over to Dupont Circle for prime people-watching or to visit the lively shops with their wide-ranging wares.

With reasonable prices and big portions, tiny Pesce is very popular. Reserve well in advance or go at off-hours.

Dupont Circle

Pesce, 2016 P St. NW (just off Dupont Circle); (202) 466-3474. Lunch Monday-Friday 11:30 a.m.-2:30 p.m., Saturday noon-2:30 p.m.; dinner Monday-Thursday 5:30-10 p.m., Friday and Saturday 5:30-10:30 p.m., Sunday 5-9:30 p.m. Metro Station: Dupont Circle.

69 / Where the Chef Knows His Onions

Vidalia

"Try the roasted onion for an appetizer; it's a signature dish and big enough for two," said the waiter. Good advice. In this restaurant called Vidalia, chef-owner Jeffrey Buben transforms Georgia's stellar Vidalia onion into a saucy treat, serving it on perky young greens in a walnut vinaigrette, along with peppered cheese, walnuts, and croutons. Buben and his wife, Sallie, also have magically turned a basement space into a beguiling country dining room and filled it with friendly, informed waiters eager to explain the food to diners wearing anything from jeans to designer suits.

Classically trained, Buben has made his name synonymous with innovative New American cuisine at various restaurants. Now he's packing in the customers with inventive dishes at his own place. Buben's food has a slight Southern accent, but don't wander in hungry for hush puppies. His emphasis is on an amalgam of new flavors to give a fresh taste to classic country goodies. Of course, some dishes are authentically Southern: The lemon chess pie and cornbread are recipes from Sallie's grandmother.

The menu changes often. For appetizers, if you opt to bypass the roasted onion, you might try Vidalia's crab cakes or charred rare tuna. Hits among the main dishes might include shrimp with thyme-accented creamed grits and caramelized onions; escalope of monkfish with wild mushroom crust in a carrot-shallot-coriander broth with spinach; or a truly sumptuous pork rib chop or pan-seared sirloin steak. For side dishes there might be succotash and garlic mashed potatoes. The daily blue-plate vegetable special is always a winner.

Desserts change daily; among the enticing treats are fresh berry sorbets and the lemon chess pie.

Dupont Circle

Vidalia, 1990 M St. NW; (202) 659-1990. Lunch Monday-Friday 11:30 a.m.-2:30 p.m., dinner Monday-Saturday 5:30-10:30 p.m. Reservations recommended. Metro Station: Dupont Circle.

70 / Rare Glimpse of Diplomatic Digs

Goodwill Embassy Tour

Unless you're invited to some official gathering, embassies generally are closed to John Q. Public. But about a dozen open their doors on a Saturday in May for those holding tickets to the annual Goodwill Embassy Tour. If you wish to be among the privileged attendees of this tour, whose proceeds have benefited disabled and disadvantaged adults for nearly fifty years, read on.

Of the 153 embassies in D.C., such a large number are concentrated on a stretch of Massachusetts Avenue on both sides of Sheridan Circle that the area is known as "Embassy Row." The Goodwill tour route takes in embassies here and wherever the hospitable may be. It also includes a stop at a mosque and tea at the Russian Orthodox Cathedral of St. Nicholas.

Ticket-holders get booklets suggesting a walking route to their destinations, but in case of inclement weather, buses shuttle tour-goers everywhere. Hostesses at each embassy meet and greet the visitors. The tour booklet provides historical background on these once-grand mansions, as well as cultural information on the countries represented by the embassies.

Tour embassies vary yearly. But rest assured that your tour will include a rich variety of countries to give you insight into several dazzling styles of diplomatic life, as well as the diverse cultures of the countries. Embassies open their dining rooms, solariums, and sometimes their living quarters. Some might serve snacks from their kitchens.

The perfect ending to this tour? Head to Adams-Morgan, Washington's most ethnically diverse neighborhood, and eat at a restaurant serving the cuisine of one of the tour's embassies.

Embassy Row

Goodwill Embassy Tour: For reservations call Davis Memorial Goodwill Industries, 2200 South Dakota Ave. NE; (202) 636-4255, ext. 1225. Recent ticket prices have been $25 to $35. Book early.

71 / Maximum Charm at Moderate Rates

The Kalorama Guest House

This four-house Victorian bed-and-breakfast (three at Kalorama Park and one at Woodley Park) is supposed to remind you of your great-grandma's attic. It's full of turn-of-the-century American antiques and period reproductions. No wonder visitors like it here: The friendly staff makes them feel right at home. Did they hear it's your birthday? You might find a balloon bouquet or celebratory cake in your room. Your anniversary? Have a bottle of champagne. Do you have questions about what to do or see? You'll get knowledgeable suggestions.

Rooms have brass or antique bedsteads, hand-me-down furniture, fresh plants, and clock radios. The rooms have no phones, but incoming calls are answered twenty-four hours a day and messages are taken efficiently. Most bathrooms have claw-foot tubs.

Continental breakfast consists of croissants, bagels, toast, and English muffins, and juice, tea, or coffee. Sherry aperitifs are free in the guests' parlors, where there are also magazines, books, and working fireplaces. There's a laundry room for guests as well as a refrigerator for ice and limited food storage.

The houses are in one of D.C.'s most interesting neighborhoods, offering many amusements for budget travelers. It costs nothing to stroll down Kalorama Road to see the Chinese and French embassies, or to explore the funky Adams-Morgan neighborhood, with antique shops, hip night spots, and more cheap restaurants than you can sample in a short visit. From the bed-and-breakfasts, it's a ten- to twenty-minute walk to the National Zoo (admission free).

Adams-Morgan

The Kalorama Guest House, 1854 Mintwood Pl. NW (between 19th St. and Columbia Rd.); (202) 667-6369; thirty-one rooms, twelve with private bath. Also, 2700 Cathedral Ave. NW; (202) 328-0860; nineteen rooms, twelve with private bath. Metro Station: Woodley Park-Zoo.

72 / Off-Beat Walking Tour with Anthony Pitch

Adams-Morgan Tour

Show up any Sunday at 11 a.m. at the Wyoming Apartment Building, 2022 Columbia Rd. NW, and Anthony Pitch will take you on a free two-hour walking tour of Adams-Morgan. Washington's answer to Greenwich Village is located in the Northwest sector, centered around 18th Street and Columbia Road. Pitch, a writer and publisher of guides and maps, was making an Adams-Morgan map for local businesses when he became so entranced that he created this free tour.

Pitch presents Adams-Morgan the way a collector might share a rare coin or prize painting. A "walking Who's Who" when it comes to famous faces behind the façades of fascinating buildings, he favors rich personal anecdotes over architectural information. His tour includes rare visits to two lobbies.

Stopping near majestic buildings and neat rows of fashionable town houses, Pitch will tell you about many former Adams-Morgan residents—including Tallulah Bankhead, Harry Truman, Dwight and Mamie Eisenhower, and the Chicago Seven's Rennie Davis—and some who live there now, such as political image-maker Frank Mankiewicz, writer Christopher Hitchins, journalist Bob Woodward, and novelist Barbara Raskin. His commentary covers current co-op prices, square footage, tips on how to get the best view of the city (pretend to be interested in buying or renting at a specific address and ask to inspect the roof), and sites moviemakers have used in well-known films.

Pitch's tour also offers a peek at Columbia Road's ethnic cafés, bars, and coffee houses, and other hangouts of the hip, new White House crowd.

Adams-Morgan

Adams-Morgan Tour, the Wyoming Apartment Building, 2022 Columbia Rd. NW; call (301) 294-9514 for information. The tour begins at 11 a.m. each Sunday outside the building, except in downpours and blizzards; free. Metro Station: Dupont Circle.

73 / A Tea to Snicker At

Four Seasons Hotel

So many celebrities stay and play at the Four Seasons; its Club Desirée guest-book signatures would fetch a fortune if auctioned. In this elegant Georgetown hotel, Marla threw one of her famous pumps at Donald; it's Demi and Bruce's place when in town. But hold on to your autograph book! The glamorous Four Seasons also gives white-glove service to kids.

"Children's tea" is served daily from 3 to 5 p.m. in the Garden Terrace (along with adults' traditional tea). And what a tea it is! Children's tea features tidbits kids dig—peanut-butter-and-jelly finger sandwiches, chocolate chip cookies, brownies, a frozen Snickers bar, chocolate-coated strawberries, and a choice of tea, milkshake, or soda—at the pint-sized price of $9.95.

Tea for little Mr. and Ms. is one facet of a family campaign at the Four Seasons, D.C.'s only five-diamond hotel. Imagine this mixture: palatial public rooms with antiques, velvet settees, Arab royalty with their retinues—and the patter of little feet.

Families receive complimentary snack packs and balloons when they check in. Video games and pool toys keep the kids amused when their parents want forty winks in their room; at night there's milk and cookies at bedtime, and special children's room service and restaurant menus are available. In the quietly elegant guest rooms and sumptuous suites, tiny tot-sized terry robes with the hotel's logo hang next to adult-sized robes. The hotel supplies cribs, little ones' toiletries, and teddy bear gifts. Kids under twelve stay free.

Want to feel like a kid again yourself? Rejuvenation awaits you at the Four Seasons' state-of-the-art fitness center. Now how about dancing till the wee hours in Club Desirée?

Georgetown

Four Seasons Hotel, 2800 Pennsylvania Ave. NW (between Rock Creek Park and 29th St.); (202) 342-0444, reservations (800) 322-3442. No nearby Metro Station, but weekday limo service downtown.

74 / Bravo-rated California Italian
Paolo's

Paolo's may not be the only restaurant in D.C. that has both a brick oven and a glassed-in kitchen, but this Georgetown spot is surely one of the most popular. That is part of the charm of this place; eating here is like enjoying a stage set with your meal. The black bar and mellow-peach-marble floors enliven one room, and wood paneling with copper accents decorates the other. A hip young crowd fills both, along with a celebrity or two (such as singer Diana Ross).

Chef Steven Roberts's engaging menu (refreshed each spring and fall) is the reason why his California Italian is still in demand. Arrive at Paolo's on a warm night, and the tables will be spilling out onto the street from the patio. Paolo's is a Restaurant Holdings restaurant; others include the wonderful Georgia Brown's and the romantic River Club. Each establishment taps into crowd-pleasing trends presented with panache.

As you study the menu, the waiter brings a tapenade (Mediterranean dip made of olives, sweet red peppers, and chick peas) with bread sticks to your table. Starters include minestrone with a hint of pesto and the deliciously crispy "beggar's purse" (a wonton wrapper fried in peanut oil and filled with wild mushrooms, spinach, and cheese). Among the pastas are fresh spinach and taleggio cheese served with roasted eggplant, wild mushrooms, and peppers; angel hair with shrimp and scallops; and black pepper linguine alla pomodoro.

The entrées include balsamic grilled chicken and a seafood mixed grill served with a saffron risotto cake. The wine list includes Italian regionals, Napa and Sonoma Valley offerings, and French champagnes.

Georgetown

Paolo's, 1303 Wisconsin Ave. NW; lunch, dinner, brunch (Saturday and Sunday); call (202) 333-7353 for hours; reservations recommended for lunch and brunch. No nearby Metro Station.

75 / Cuisine Courant from California, on the C&O

Citronelle

It's foodies-and-famous gridlock all the time at Citronelle, the highly praised restaurant featuring Chef Michel Richard's innovative cooking. If you want to get in, reserve far in advance.

Acclaimed in Los Angeles for his expensive restaurant Citron, Richard opened this somewhat-less-expensive version, Citronelle, in Georgetown. He trained Chef Etienne Jaulin to prepare his cuisine—a blend of Richard's French background and California influences that results in delightfully light dishes.

The restaurant's setting is cheerful, airy, and indeed Californialike. The dining rooms have dark green wicker chairs, contemporary prints on the walls, and strategically placed plants. The focal point is a showcase kitchen, where chefs and preppers turn out outstanding meals. Guests are well dressed in business/dressy clothes (evening) and service is very nice.

The menu changes frequently but is reliably delicious—an imaginative mingling of earthy and elegant. For an appetizer you might try the sautéed foie gras with chanterelles, or crab cannelloni, or a salmon or artichoke terrine. Entrées that have been great successes include rare tuna chateaubriand, rockfish on saffron-seasoned pasta, rabbit and lentils, and roasted lobster.

Desserts include such Richard calling cards as caramel napoleon, and chocolate hazelnut bars. The wine list has a good selection of American labels, and its selections are expensive. In addition to à la carte, there are prix fixe menus. The three-course prix fixe lunch, $16.50, is a fabulous find.

Citronelle is in The Latham, an elegant, small hotel with lovely rooms, with some canal views.

Georgetown

Citronelle, 3000 M St. NW; (202) 625-2150. Lunch every day 11:30 a.m.-2 p.m.; dinner Sunday-Thursday 6-10 p.m., Saturday 5:30-10:30 p.m. Hotel (202) 726-5000; reservations 800-Latham-1.

76 / Elegance Alert: Delicious Art Deco in Georgetown

The River Club

Making the journey from a lane in Georgetown through the etched glass doors to the art deco River Club is like boarding a time machine. It is easy to believe you've entered a 1930s night club. Will they be drinking bathtub gin out of teacups?

In two words: no way. The River Club boasts some of the best champagnes in the city, including several têtes de cuvées (best champagnes for their year); and it also serves top-notch Burgundies and Bordeaux. The food is first rate, too.

With a fifty-foot serpentine bar, ten-foot glass-etched waterfall, Ertes-inspired paintings, and romantic lighting, the elegant River Club is not the place for backward baseball caps and cut-offs. People dress up to dine and dance the night away to jazz piano and Sinatra-Bennett tunes until 9 p.m. and a deejay after that. They kick up their heels to live music during Wednesday's "Night in Rio" or Thursday's "Return to an Era."

There's a pages-long wine list to study while deciding what to eat, and vintage people-watching when dancers twirl past your table. Chef Mark Simon's menu, refreshed four times a year, blends New American with retro (steak Diane). The most popular dishes are the smoked lobster, served with crispy spinach and stir-fried vegetables, and grilled swordfish steak in a Dijon mustard sauce; but the steak Diane with mustard and Cognac sauce and the pan-roasted breast of duck also have their fans. For starters, try grilled jumbo shrimp wrapped in prosciutto, especially delicious with mango compote or the caviar (beluga; $70).

Desserts include a velvety crème brûlée and a luscious chocolate pistachio cake. *Georgetown*

The River Club, 3223 K St. NW (between Cecil Pl. and Wisconsin Ave.); (202) 333-8118. Dinner 7 p.m.-midnight; dancing until the wee hours on Friday and Saturday. Reservations recommended. No nearby Metro Station.

77 / Georgetown Behind-the-Scenes Tours

Georgetown Houses/Garden Tour

About the time the last cherry blossom has drifted down, Washingtonians turn to two tours, little known to tourists, that open the doors to some of Georgetown's most exclusive houses and gardens. Here's the information you need to join the insiders on these exclusive excursions. Dates vary from year to year, but the months remain the same. Book well in advance.

Planning an April visit? For almost sixty years, the two-day Georgetown House Tour, a fund-raiser for historic St. John's church, has taken place in mid- to late-April. (Recent admission: $20 per ticket.) Tour houses vary yearly, but the tour always offers a rare chance to see some fabulous interiors. Recently, the tour included famous Federalist, Georgian, and Victorian houses; an author's aerie penthouse; houses with smashing views; and, as added attractions, two unusual chapels. Tour-goers take tea at St. John's, built in 1809, where Thomas Jefferson was a leading parishioner and Francis Scott Key a vestryman.

Expecting to be in town in May? The Georgetown Children's House Garden Tour has been delighting people for more than sixty years. This tour benefits the Georgetown Children's House, which provides essential services to children of low-income working families. (Recent ticket prices: $12-$15.) Like the house tour, the garden tour's sites vary, but always include a variety of motifs in a dozen gardens. They might range from a tiny garden inspired by Beatrix Potter's *Tale of Peter Rabbit*, to the brilliant four-acre Italianate gardens at Evermay, one of Georgetown's grandest mansions. Light refreshments wind up the day. *Georgetown*

Georgetown House Tours: For information, contact St. John's Episcopal Church, 3240 Q St. NW (between Potomac St. and Wisconsin Ave.); (202) 338-1796.

Garden Tour: For information, contact Children's House, 3224 N St. NW; (202) 333-4953. No nearby Metro Station.

78 / Go Back to the Nineteenth Century

Chesapeake & Ohio Canal Barge Tours

Escape the mundane with an unusual trip back to the nineteenth century on the Chesapeake & Ohio (C&O) Canal. When opened in 1850, the seventy-four-lock canal linked Georgetown to Cumberland, Maryland. (The goal never realized was Pittsburgh, Pennsylvania.)

The canal was doomed from the start; the day of the ground-breaking in 1828, construction also began on the Baltimore & Ohio railway, which eventually put the C&O out of business. (The canal operated until 1914.) Today, the C&O is a National Park. Guides in period costumes conduct ninety-minute voyages for passengers between mid-April and October aboard the *Georgetown*.

You begin your journey by sitting in the barge below street level while rangers open one of the locks and maneuver the sturdy craft through the rising waters. When you reach the tow path, your barge is hitched to a mule and proceeds to travel at a leisurely three miles per hour.

During the trip, rangers use folk tunes to conjure the past, tell tall tales, and conduct occasional quizzes aimed especially at kids. You can picnic aboard, but you might prefer to wait until after the trip and hike to one of those out-of-the-way nooks beyond Georgetown.

The tow path still extends 184 miles to Cumberland and is open all year long. You can hike, bike, or horseback ride on the tow path, or join one of the National Park Service guided hikes into rugged terrain.

Georgetown

Chesapeake & Ohio Canal Barge Tours, 1055 Thomas Jefferson St. NW; (202) 472-4376. Wednesday-Sunday 10:30 a.m., 1 and 3 p.m., Saturday 10:30 a.m. and 1, 3, and 5 p.m. In Great Falls, Maryland, departures are in front of the Great Falls Tavern; (301) 299-2026. Admission $5 for adults, $3.50 for seniors and children under thirteen.

79 / Picturesque Walk

Georgetown

Georgetown, D.C.'s oldest neighborhood, was a thriving tobacco port in the late 1700s; by the mid-1840s it was an insalubrious industrial district. Rediscovered by newcomers in the 1940s, its Georgian, Federal, and Victorian homes are occupied by today's lords and ladies of D.C. The narrow tree-shaded streets are made for meandering; but where to go and what to see? Two free maps offer walking tours to the highlights of Georgetown.

The *Washington Street Map and Visitors' Guide,* available at several locations (see below), describes various D.C. walking tours; Georgetown concentrates on the swanky upper portion (see Dumbarton Oaks, page 87, and Tudor Place, page 88).

In lower Georgetown, the tiny buildings lining narrow streets once were workers' homes and now are fashionable residences, chic shops, and hip eateries. At the Old Stone House (M Street between 30th and 31st streets), you can pick up a brochure that not only describes the house but also includes a map for a lower-Georgetown walking tour.

Be sure to look around the Old Stone House, believed to be the only surviving pre-Revolutionary War building in D.C. Cabinet-maker Christopher Layman built the little kitchen (1764), and Cassandra Crew added a second-floor kitchen and third-floor bedroom (1767). The adjoining garden is a delight; it is planted with fruit trees and flowers of bygone days. The property is maintained by the National Park Service, and guides in costumes are on hand to answer questions: 3051 M St. NW (between 30th and 31st streets); (202) 426-6851. Wednesday-Sunday 8 a.m.-4:30 p.m. No nearby Metro Station.

The *Washington Street Map and Visitors' Guide* is available at Traveler's Aid in Union Station and at many hotels; drivers can find it in the Virginia and Maryland Welcome Centers.

Georgetown

80 / Political Antics

Chelsea's/The Capitol Steps

Suppose your boss does something stupid and instead of gossiping about it at the office, you hire a hall and tell everyone.

This is what happens at Chelsea's every Friday and Saturday night, when the Capitol Steps, a group of former and current Congressional aides, perform their musical political satire.

The Capitol Steps started as a joke in 1981 at a Christmas party in Senator Charles Percy's office. Now the group brings its rapier-sharp bits to NPR and CNN as well as organizations nationwide.

Pols are roasted most. Bill Clinton is portrayed as a guitar-toting, hip-wiggling Elvis. Ross Perot pesters when least expected. Bob Dole begs for love.

Much of the fun comes from the fact that the troupe's squeaky-clean looks are entirely at odds with their wicked lyrics, as is their penchant for setting those lyrics to well-worn tunes.

Lorena Bobbitt sings about severance pay to "Bibbity-Bobbity-Boo." Jesse Helms croons to "Chattanooga Choo-Choo": "Pardon me boys, but give the statue here a tutu. . . ." To the tune "Camelot," Saddam Hussein belts out "My Camel Lot."

An audience favorite, "Lirty Dies" (Dirty Lies), changes the first letters of words ("skex sandals" for "sex scandals") to get away with telling risqué tales.

Indeed, the name Capitol Steps refers to a "skex sandal"—Congressman John Jenrette and wife Rita's ballyhooed moonlight trysting place. Chelsea's is also D.C.'s headquarters for spicy Latin rhythms from a live band. On some nights, there's live Persian music.

Georgetown

Chelsea's, 1055 Thomas Jefferson St. NW (between K and M streets); (202) 298-8222.

The Capitol Steps, Friday at 8 p.m., Saturday at 7:30 p.m.; Latin nights, Thursday-Saturday, 11 p.m.-3 a.m.; Persian nights, Wednesday and Sunday, 9:30 p.m.-2 a.m. No nearby Metro Station.

81 / Resting Places in Georgetown
Oak Hill Cemetery and Montrose Park

This excursion combines a walk to Georgetown's beautiful old Oak Hill Cemetery with a picnic in quiet Montrose Park. Less spectacular than Arlington National Cemetery, Oak Hill is nonetheless of interest historically and architecturally.

Start in the Dupont Circle area with a stop at Burrito Bros. (1524 Connecticut Ave. NW) to buy a taco or burrito ($3-$4) for your lunch in Montrose Park. (No picnicking is permitted in the cemetery.) Walk along Q Street west to Bison Bridge (mistakenly called Buffalo). Named for its four bronze bison the bridge crosses Rock Creek into Georgetown. Look over the sides to see the Native American busts by Glenn Brown and son Bedford, who designed the bridge in 1914.

Turn right and walk up to R Street to Oak Hill Cemetery. At the gatehouse you can buy a brochure that shows where notables are buried, or you can just wander the paths.

Oak Hill, built on terraces declining toward Rock Creek Park, was founded in 1849 by financier/philanthropist William Wilson Corcoran, whose art collection established the Corcoran Gallery of Art. He is buried here, and so are many other notable Americans, including John Howard Payne, composer of "Home Sweet Home," and statesmen Edward Stanton, James G. Blaine, and Dean Acheson. Inscriptions on the headstones reveal both prominent and plain permanent Washingtonians. The 1849 gate house and the Gothic chapel, built in 1850, are by James Renwick, designer of the Smithsonian "Castle."

Next door is small, woodsy Montrose Park for your picnic. Lover's Lane separates this park from Dumbarton Oaks (see page 87).

Georgetown

Oak Hill Cemetery and Montrose Park, 30th and R streets NW; (202) 337-2835. Open weekdays 10 a.m.-4 p.m.; closed major holidays. Metro Station: Dupont Circle, then walk as directed.

82 / Have a First-Class, Secondhand Day

Fabulous Fashions, Books, and Other Buys

The Armanis and Hugo Bosses in D.C. resale and secondhand shops may have made recent appearances at a White House "do" or cabinet meeting when new; try the other stores for retro looks, hard-to-find books, and quirky souvenirs.

Cheap, Chic Threads *Secondhand Rose,* 1516 Wisconsin Ave. NW, between P and O streets; (202) 337-3378; no nearby Metro Station, stocks women's like-new contemporary ready-to-wear. Georgetown. *Once Is Not Enough* 4830 MacArthur Blvd. NW, at Reservoir Rd.; (202) 332-3072; no nearby Metro Station, is where the well-to-do send their up-to-the-minute fashions for resale. *Secondi* 1611 Connecticut Ave. NW, 2nd floor; (202) 667-1122; Metro Station: Farragut West, is a consignment boutique that features designer fashions for both men and women. *A Man for All Seasons* 321 Seventh St. SE, between Pennsylvania Ave. and P St.; (202) 544-4432; Metro Station: Eastern Market, stocks savvy secondhand fashions for thrifty, quality-conscious men.

Vintage Wear *Circa 1940,* 1608 20th St. NW; (202) 332-9211; Metro Station: Dupont Circle, is a must-stop for retro apparel for both men and women, custom-tailored suits, haberdashery, formal wear, and bridal gowns.

Books *Second Story,* 2000 P St. NW, at 20th St.; (202) 659-8884; Metro Station: Dupont Circle, is the best spot in D.C. for used rare, old, and out-of-print books at affordable prices. Also carries vintage posters and other collectibles. Branches in Bethesda and Rockville, Maryland. *Booked Up* 1209 31st St. NW, between M and N streets; (202) 965-3244; no nearby Metro Station, specializes in antiquarian century-spanning editions. Author Larry McMurtry (*Lonesome Dove*) owns this bookstore.

Georgetown

83 / See the Big Game

Washington's Popular Sports Bars

The odds of you beating out local fans and getting regular-price tickets to a Redskins game are about the same as those for becoming president. Anyone can do it, but few actually do. But yes, you can still see the "Big Game"—at one of D.C.'s many sports bars. Following are a few choice spots.

Champions is a well-known Georgetown sports bar. The decor features walls hung with sports stars' photos, jerseys, and other paraphernalia, and Redskins and Capitols team players drop in here. The big-screen TV is permanently fixed on the game du jour. In the early evening, the clientele is over thirty; after 11 p.m., a younger crowd takes over. Serves burgers, wings, and other similar foods. One-drink minimum.

Jenkins Hill Pub, near Capitol Hill, attracts young Hill staffers with its clubby atmosphere, turn-of-the-century stained glass, and two TV sets flanking the bar, perpetually tuned to ESPN. Upstairs there's a giant TV for sports fans, pool tables, and a dart board. Menu selections include pizza, burgers, pasta, and salads.

Bottom Line's owners—Dick Heidenberger and Jack Million—were rugby players, so this sports bar attracts rugby fans. Other athletes drop in periodically. Stop by for Monday's game on TV and get a free hot dog. Tuesday through Saturday, a deejay spins dance music after 9 p.m.; this is also the home of the "wacky-but-harmless" stunt. Light menu; sandwiches, salads, that sort of thing.

Champions, 1206 Wisconsin Ave. NW; (202) 965-4005; Monday-Thursday 5 p.m.-2 a.m., Friday 5 p.m.- 2:30 a.m., Saturday and Sunday 11 a.m.-2:30 a.m. No nearby Metro Station.

Jenkins Hill Pub, 319 Pennsylvania Ave. SE; (202) 544-6600; Monday-Saturday 11:30 a.m.-1:30 a.m. Metro Station: Capitol South.

Bottom Line, 1716 I St. NW; (202) 298-8488; Monday-Thursday 11:30 a.m.-1:30 a.m., Friday and Saturday 11:30 a.m.-2:30 a.m. Metro Station: Farragut West.

84 / Shopping Break

Georgetown Park

Georgetown Park may be the only shopping center with its own museum: it is definitely the only one that segues into a national park, the Chesapeake & Ohio National Park.

Georgetown Park's assortment of shops in a picturesque setting has become a mecca for upscale shoppers. Local people shop here, and the Old Town Trolleys discharge tourists from all points.

Opened in 1981, the mall was built into what had been both an old tobacco warehouse and trolley car barn (check out the on-site museum in space 236 for details). The decor is high Victorian, with palms, fountains, frosted glass, and statuary.

Four levels of shops, more than one hundred altogether, encircle an airy plant- and pool-filled atrium; shops on the upper levels peek out through brass-and-iron balconies. Evergreens and tiny lights twine through the balconies from December 1-January 1, when the mall is decked out for the holidays.

Georgetown Park mixes well-known specialty shops (Ann Taylor, Polo/Ralph Lauren) with entrepreneurs trying new ideas. The Department of the Interior's Indian Craft Shop has concha belts and kachina dolls; Fire and Ice sells minerals as jewelry and in orbs and obelisks; Gallery of History has autographed artifacts, and Paso Real Gallery specializes in papier-mâché.

For eats, Georgetown Park has Dean & DeLuca for espresso and light fare; Clyde's, a turn-of-the-century-inspired saloon serving burgers and crab cakes; and restaurants for Italian, Japanese, or deli dishes.

Afterward, step out the C&O entrance to a national park.

Georgetown

Georgetown Park, 3222 M Street NW (near Wisconsin Ave.); (202) 298-5577. Monday-Saturday 10 a.m.-6 p.m., Sunday noon-6 p.m. Restaurant hours vary. No nearby Metro Station.

85 / Splendor in the Grass

Dumbarton Oaks

Six miles from the Capitol, in upper Georgetown, is Dumbarton Oaks, a choice place for a relaxing afternoon. The handsome neo-Georgian mansion capping the hill is renowned as the site where the foundation of the United Nations Charter was laid in 1944; it also inspired Igor Stravinsky's Concerto in E Flat (Dumbarton Oaks Concerto). The composer himself performed it here for the thirtieth anniversary of Mr. and Mrs. Robert Woods Bliss.

Built in 1801, the mansion was remodeled in 1921 when Bliss, a career diplomat, and his wife, Mildred, heir to the Fletcher's Castoria fortune, purchased it. In 1940, they gave their estate to Harvard University, which maintains the Blisses' small but noteworthy collection of Byzantine and pre-Columbian art.

Below the mansion are the magnificently orchestrated ten-acre formal gardens designed by Beatrix Farrand and Mildred Bliss. The two well-traveled women translated the great garden traditions of Italy, France, and England to create a wonderland of interconnected "garden rooms" layered onto the hillside.

When the Blisses were here, the terraces and lawns of Dumbarton Oaks were alive with world glitterati. Then, as now, of the eighteen separate gardens, especially beloved has been the geometrically precise Rose Garden, with flowers rainbowing from ivory to crimson; viewed from the Urn Garden, the roses appear to be framed paintings. Perhaps the most unusual creation is the Pebble Garden Fountain, with stone mosaics sparkling with water. This garden is equally beautiful in every season.

Georgetown

Dumbarton Oaks, 1703 32nd St. NW (garden entrance at 31st and R streets NW); (202) 338-8278. Open daily April-October 2-6 p.m. and November-March 2-5 p.m. Admission $3. Self-guided tour map at entrance. Art collection open 2-5 p.m. Tuesday-Sunday; rare book room open 2-5 p.m. weekends. No nearby Metro Station. Walk over Bison (Dumbarton) Bridge to Q Street and head north to R Street, or take a taxi.

86 / Take a History Break

Tudor Place

The misleadingly named Tudor Place is actually a lovely neoclassical-style mansion—a "must" for history, architecture, and gardening buffs. Designed by Capitol architect William Thornton, Tudor Place was completed in 1816 for Thomas Peter, son of the first mayor of Georgetown, and his wife, Martha "Patsy" Custis, granddaughter of Martha Washington. Succeeding generations of this family lived here until 1983, when Armistead Peter III died. He and his wife, Caroline, set up the foundation that restored the property, opened it to the public in 1988, and maintains it.

The lemon-colored stucco house has an interesting two-story domed portico on the south side. Its interiors are even more fascinating. Because of its tie to Martha Washington, Tudor Place has many objects from Mount Vernon—among them, chairs that belonged to George Washington; Francis Scott Key's desk; and spurs of those in the Peters family who perished in the Civil War. In the elegant double parlors, where the family entertained such notables as Henry Clay and Daniel Webster, you'll meet the daughters of the original household through candy-box-pretty portraiture.

Expansive lawns, parterres, and woodlands date from the Federal period of the original householders; each successive generation has added to the garden. Some trees date from the nineteenth century. The shrubs, flowers, and intricate flower knot design recall earlier days, as do the famous roses. The ever-blooming China rose "Old Blush," along the south façade is said to have been planted by Martha Peters herself.

Georgetown

Tudor Place, 1644 31st St. NW; (south of Dumbarton Oaks); (202) 965-0400. Tours at 10 and 11:30 a.m., 1 and 2:30 p.m. Admission: $7.50 (includes garden). Reservations recommended, but drop-ins are welcome. Ring bell at gate. No nearby Metro Station.

87 / Treats for Everyone

Delicious Dishes and Where to Find Them

Aditi   Creamy walls and fresh flowers accompany well-prepared inexpensive Indian food in a quiet Georgetown duplex, 3299 M. St. NW; (202) 625-6825; lunch and dinner, Tuesday-Sunday; no nearby Metro Station.

 Belmont Kitchen   Small, trendy contemporary café in Adams-Morgan; delicious upside-down pizza, 2400 18th St. NW, at Belmont Rd.; (202) 667-1200; lunch and dinner; Metro Station: Woodley Park-Zoo.

 Bob's Famous Homemade Ice Cream   A former barrister turned ice-cream maven offers plain and fancy flavors, 236 Massachusetts Ave. NE, between 2nd and 3rd streets; (202) 546-3860; daily 7:30 a.m.-11 p.m.; Metro Station: Union Station.

 Booeymonger   Delicious Dagwood-size sandwiches for under $5; eat-in/take-out; try the cinnamon coffee, 3265 Prospect St. NW at Potomac St.; (202) 333-4810; another location in Friendship Heights; no nearby Metro Station: Georgetown.

 Gerard's Place   Two-star Michelin chef Gerard Pangaud lives up to his reputation with affordable luxury cuisine. (Five-course tasting menu: $50.) Surprise your tastebuds, 915 15th St. NW; (202) 737-4445; Monday-Friday lunch and dinner, Saturday dinner; Metro Station: McPherson Square.

 La Tomate   Inventive budget pasta dishes; white, airy interior with big windows; and an outdoor café for people-watching. Daffy service, 1701 Connecticut Ave. NW, at R St.; (202) 667-5505; lunch and dinner; Metro Station: Dupont Circle.

 Palais du Chocolat   Chocolate gets the royal treatment. Superlative cakes, pastries, croissants; 3309 Connecticut Ave. NW; (202) 363-2462; open every day, 8 a.m. till 10:30 p.m. weekdays, later on weekends; Metro Station: Cleveland Park.

 The Dancing Crab   Famous fresh Maryland crab in many guises; all-you-can-eat crab feasts in summer, $15, 4611 Wisconsin Ave. NW; (202) 244-1882; Metro Station: Tenleytown.

88 / D.C.'s Hottest Jazz Club

Blues Alley

Washington's monument to jazz is Blues Alley, which claims to be the nation's oldest continuous jazz supper club. Certainly, it is one of the most internationally well known and popular. Overseas visitors (including Czech President Vaclav Havel), as well as those from across the fifty states, seek it out specially to hear some of the world's jazz greats in an intimate setting.

Blues Alley strives for the ambience of a hot 1920s jazz spot. Located in an eighteenth-century Georgetown carriage house, the club is a dimly lit, 124-seat hideaway with exposed brick windowless walls hung with photos of stars who have performed there over the years. Jazz greats have included Ella Fitzgerald, Dizzy Gillespie, Sarah Vaughan, Ahmad Jamal, Lou Rawls, Nancy Wilson, and Wynton Marsalis (usually Marsalis's Christmas gig); an occasional Broadway star/cabaret performer such as Karen Akers makes an appearance, too.

Blues Alley focused on Dixieland and blues singers when it opened in 1965; the emphasis has shifted to jazz over the years. But the name is unchanged, and in 1982, the alley in which the club is located was officially named "Blues Alley."

Although Blues Alley is a jazz supper club, food plays second fiddle to the music here; however, diners get preferred tables at showtime. (In such intimate quarters, any table is good, as are the barstools.) The menu features Creole fare, steaks and chops, and late-night snacks.

After their shows, artists usually hang out at the bar to talk with fans; tapes that have been recorded on site are for sale.

Georgetown

Blues Alley, 1073 Wisconsin Ave. NW; (202) 337-4141. Shows Monday-Thursday and Sunday 8 and 10 p.m., Friday and Saturday 8 and 10 p.m. and midnight. Reservations recommended; required for some shows. No nearby Metro Station.

89 / Where Elvis Reigns

Old Glory's BBQ

Seeking the soothing effects of rich barbecued ribs and the balm of fresh catfish and hush puppies? Then head straight for Old Glory in Georgetown. For some time now, an eclectic mixture of Dixie transplants homesick for Southern food, assorted hearty eaters, and Generation X'ers looking for soul mates have made this spicy morsel their headquarters, even if it means lining up to get in. Others come here to pay homage to Elvis, whose statue is prominent behind the bar.

This is a place to dress as you please, have great fun with friends, and enjoy the open-pit barbecue and tongue-in-chic decor. Nibble on an order of oak-fired chicken wings while checking out the room.

Old Glory's funky ambience combines roadside diner kitsch with a theme park motif. The restaurant flies the flags of six states: Tennessee, Texas, Georgia, Arkansas, and North and South Carolina; gracing the tables are six state-named barbecue sauces.

The restaurant's menu ranges over their barbecue specialties: pork and beef ribs, pulled (shredded) pork and chicken, fried catfish with hush puppies, smoked Virginia ham, smoked chicken, and so forth, often with an unusual twist in a sauce or seasoning. Open-pit-roasted vegetables are a tasty dish for non-meat-eaters.

Platters combining different entrées served with side dishes such as mustard slaw and hoppin' John (combination of black-eyed peas and rice) are a good value at around $14, and are about the highest-priced items on the menu.

Skip the wine. Whatever your main dish, one of the lagers or ales goes best with it; or you can try root beer on tap.

Georgetown

Old Glory, 3139 M St. NW; (202) 337-3406. Lunch and dinner Monday-Thursday 11:30 a.m.-11:30 p.m., Friday and Saturday 11:30 a.m.-12:30 a.m., Sunday 11 a.m.-11 p.m. Reservations for groups of eight or more. No nearby Metro Station.

90 / Have a Wild Time

D.C.'s Wonderful Parks

Don't retreat to your hotel room to escape the hubbub. You can get away from the city without ever leaving it.

The parks of Washington, D.C. are great getaways. How about a 185-mile-long canal with bordering trail (see C&O Canal, page 80). and thousands of miles of untamed wilderness right in the center of the city? Or an 88-acre wilderness preserve on the Potomac River? Here are a few of the ways to go wild in D.C. (see also More Wild Times, page 103).

Rock Creek Park, a remarkable eighteen-hundred-acre ribbon of green on either side of Rock Creek, starts at the Potomac River and extends to Montgomery County, Maryland. A getaway for Washingtonians since the 1800s, this gargantuan park has a multiplicity of activities; an extensive area of beautiful wooded hiking, jogging, and biking trails; a nineteenth-century water-driven gristmill and carriage house turned into an art gallery; 30 picnic areas; playgrounds; sports facilities, such as 15 soft-clay tennis courts and 10 hard-surface courts, as well as an 18-hole golf course, riding stables, and boating; a gargantuan outdoor theater (see Carter Barron Amphitheater, page 25); a planetarium; and a host of programs for all ages. These include guided nature walks, as you might expect, but also poetry reading and workshops. Other unusual attractions in Rock Creek Park include the remnants of forts that defended Washington, D.C. during the Civil War. For details, visit the Rock Creek Nature Center, where there are numerous on-site activities. For general information about activities, and to reserve a tennis court, picnic area, or other facility, visit or call the park's headquarters.

Upper Northwest

Rock Creek Nature Center, 5200 Glover Rd.; (202) 426-6829. Wednesday-Sunday 9 a.m.-5 p.m.; closed federal holidays.

Park Headquarters, 5000 Glover Rd.; (202) 426-6832. Monday-Friday 7:45 a.m.-4:15 p.m.

91 / Hotel with Kids' Concierges

Omni Shoreham Hotel

There was a time when JFK courted Jackie in the Blue Room, where Judy Garland and Frank Sinatra starred; when the "mostest" hostess Perle Mesta threw parties here and King Saud tipped the staff with solid-gold watches. Inaugural balls are still held at the Omni Shoreham, as they have been since FDR's day.

Who are the newest VIPs? Kids—at least on summer weekends. There's a "Kids' concierge," namely, a Washington-area youngster who can brief visiting children on area attractions. These lures include two swimming pools and a host of other recreational activities on fourteen acres of adjacent Rock Creek Park and the nearby zoo. Kids also get gifts and discounts in shops. The family weekend package costs $99 a night for a deluxe room; kids seventeen and under can stay free in parents' room. A free video and a pizza for four are part of the package.

Not everybody is a kid, of course; rest assured that pleasures for grown-ups abound at the Omni Shoreham as well, including other weekend bargain rates. Built in the 1930s in the art deco-Renaissance style, the hotel's marvelous public rooms have been refurbished to their glory days. Especially wonderful is the lobby, a fascinating mixture of artifacts, polished marble, vaulted ceilings, and crystal chandeliers. Half of the spacious, tasteful guest rooms overlook the park.

The hotel's Monique Café et Brasserie, with its red lacquer frame mirrors, palms, and dark woods, might be in Montparnasse. Selections on the menu include classic brasserie fare such as steak au poivre and rotisserie-cooked meats. The palm-studded Garden Court is welcoming for drinks after a harried sightseeing day. And when it's time to step out, there's the art-deco Marquee nightclub for political satire and jazz.

Upper Northwest

Omni Shoreham Hotel, 2500 Calvert St. NW; (202) 234-0700; (800) THE-OMNI. Metro Station: Woodley Park-Zoo.

92 / See Walls That Speak

Washington's Wonderful Murals

Mention Washington, D.C. to almost anyone, and marble monuments come to mind. But keep your eyes open and you'll be entertained and surprised by the city's big, bright, bold story-telling murals. Some have been privately financed and others are carried out by D.C. Art/Works, in cooperation with the D.C. Commission on the Arts and Humanities. Appearing in a variety of spaces, from soup kitchens and shelters to banks and restaurants, the murals add vibrancy everywhere.

At Woodley Park in upper northwest D.C., amid elegant row houses and cafés, and not far from the Omni Shoreham Hotel, is possibly the most famous D.C. mural—a super-size portrait of Marilyn Monroe. Privately commissioned, this mural by John Bailey is on the south wall of Salon Roi, 2602 Connecticut Ave. NW. Metro Station: Woodley Park-Zoo.

Also in upper northwest D.C., a retaining wall mural (Adams Mill Road at Calvert Street NW) swoops up to five feet in a colorful Latin American life scene. This mural was designed by Jorge Luis Somarriba and painted by youngsters from the Latin American Youth Center. Metro Station: Woodley Park-Zoo.

Nearby in funky Adams-Morgan, there are a number of delightful murals on cafés and shops. The most outstanding is a D.C. Art/Works mural on the back wall of the old Ontario Theater (Columbia and Ontario roads NW) showing two colorful macaws and a multicultural setting by G. Byron Peck. Metro Station: DuPont Circle.

In the northeast, at Benning Park Community Center (53rd and Fitch streets), Rod Turner's mural shows a family dinner with mythic figures of African-American leaders.

Downtown, Val Lewton's mural on a one-hundred-foot-high air shaft (2nd and H streets and Massachusetts Ave. NW) gives the illusion of looking through a hole at the Capitol.

Keep looking; you'll see many more.

93 / Tea in Angel Territory

Washington National Cathedral

D.C.'s most unusual spot for tea is the Washington National Cathedral's Observation Gallery, at the highest point in the city. Tea is served on Tuesdays and Wednesdays following a special 1:30 p.m. tour ($15); you'll share the heavenly view with the 388 angels carved around the cathedral's thirty-story central carillon tower. Washingtonians love to surprise visitors by taking them here; make your reservations up to two months in advance.

Officially the Cathedral Church of St. Peter and St. Paul, it is built in the Gothic style with flying buttresses, transepts, and barrel vaults that were constructed block by block without structural steel. The cathedral took eighty-three years to complete. In 1907 Teddy Roosevelt laid the foundation stone using the same silver trowel George Washington had used when laying the cornerstone of the Capitol, and the structure was finished in 1990, becoming the world's sixth-largest cathedral. This Episcopal church welcomes worshipers of all denominations.

More than two hundred stained-glass windows line the ten-story nave. Among the gems are the West Rose Window, made of twelve hundred pieces of glass that look incendiary at sunset; and the Space Window, displaying a moon rock given to the cathedral by the Apollo XI astronauts.

Woodrow Wilson and his second wife, Edith, are buried here; Wilson is the only president buried in Washington, D.C.

To one side of the main altar in the charming children's chapel; everything is tots' size. Beautiful needlepoint designs cover the chapel's kneelers.

The 57-acre grounds house both the Herb Cottage and Bishop's Garden in medieval style.

Upper Northwest

Washington National Cathedral, bounded by Wisconsin and Massachusetts avenues NW and 34th and Garfield streets; (202) 537-6200. Open 10 a.m.-4:30 p.m. Monday-Saturday, 7:30 a.m.-4:30 p.m. Sundays. No nearby Metro Station; take Metrobus 30, 32, 34, or 36.

94 / Roam Among Animals

National Zoological Park

How does an urban zoo make itself enjoyable and educational to kids at the same time?

The answer at the National Zoological Park is to make learning fun. Here kids can not only see exotic animals, but become pint-size zoologists by participating in a variety of learning labs.

At the Education Center near the Connecticut Avenue entrance, visitors can get information on labs as well as maps of the 163-acre handsomely landscaped zoo. Designed in 1889 by Frederick Law Olmsted, the zoo is under the direction of the Smithsonian. It is a state-of-the-art showplace for five thousand animals of some five hundred species, many rare and/or endangered, housed in naturalistic surroundings. Six trails of stenciled footprints mark paths to the animals' compounds.

The zoo's most popular resident is the giant panda, Hsing-Hsing (Bright Star), a gift in 1972 from the People's Republic of China (feeding times: 11 a.m. and 3 p.m.). Be advised that Hsing-Hsing sleeps a lot. He is not into crowd-pleasing antics as are some of the tenants in the Great Ape House.

Youngsters learn while visiting the zoo not only by observing the animals but through attractive graphics and games. Sketches show visitors how far cheetahs can jump; a scale shows how a small visitor's weight compares to that of a snack for a great jungle cat. The little touches like these make this zoo special to children.

The zoo has a wonderful walk-in aviary where birds fly unrestricted. The invertebrate exhibit is unique in this country, and so are the Komodo dragons.

Upper Northwest

National Zoological Park, 3001 Connecticut Ave. NW; (202) 673-4800. Daily, May 1-September 15: buildings 9 a.m.-6 p.m., grounds 8 a.m.-8 p.m. Remainder of the year: buildings 9 a.m.-4 p.m., grounds 8 a.m.-6 p.m.; free. Cafés, picnic areas, shops, stroller rental stations. Metro Station: Woodley Park-Zoo.

95 / Russian Treasures
Hillwood Museum

To experience a Russian art collection unparalleled in the U.S., visit Marjorie Merriweather Post's mansion, Hillwood, in Northwest D.C. True, you reach Hillwood via the Metro, but once there, the Russian art, French furnishings, and lovely gardens make this huge estate seem far removed from the hectic world.

Post (1887-1973), the cereal heiress, acquired her 1920s-built forty-room mansion in 1955 and renovated it with an eye toward opening it to the public. As a museum since 1977, its sense of grandeur has dazzled visitors. The mansion looks today as it did when Post lived here, and it provides a glimpse at a life of glamor and luxury.

Among the Russian treasures are dinner plates commissioned by Catherine the Great and ninety objects by Peter Carl Fabergé, including jewel-encrusted eggs, clocks, and boxes. Post acquired these and other treasures after the Russian Revolution when she was in that country with her third husband, Joseph E. Davies, first U.S. ambassador to the Soviet Union.

Among the ornate Hillwood furnishings are eighteenth-century French tapestries, furniture, and Sèvres porcelain. Post's elegant gowns, elaborate jewelry, and lavish lace collection are also on view.

The twenty-five-acre grounds mix French and Japanese garden styles with winding paths, pools, and wooded areas studded with azaleas, laurels, and rhododendrons.

The estate also includes a dacha (small Russian country house) and the Native American Building.

Upper Northwest

Hillwood Museum, 4155 Linnean Ave. NW; (202) 686-5807. House and grounds tour ($10) Tuesday-Saturday. Requires reservations; call far in advance. Children under twelve not permitted on house tour. Garden-only tour: grounds open 11 a.m.-3 p.m. Closed in February and on holidays. Metro Station: Van Ness-UDC; then a one-mile walk. Note: Taxis often have trouble finding Hillwood.

96 / Antique Shopping Spree

Kensington, Maryland

Forty small shops featuring fine antiques and collectibles in a village setting known as Antique Village put a trip to Kensington high on the agenda for collectors and inveterate shoppers. Better yet, the village gets relatively few tourist shoppers because quiet Kensington is one of the few suburbs not directly served by Metro. (Note: it is an easy bus or car trip.) Antique Village offers gifts for everyone on your list, as well as for your own collection. How about a glass rolling pin? A crystal chandelier for $3,500? A china-face doll? A lovely rosewood table?

Some shops in the several buildings sell only authentic antiques, and others blend the old with new items made to look old. "Charming copy of an old piece," the salesperson said about a delicate necklace. Generally, salespeople seemed well-informed and forthcoming about merchandise's pedigrees or lack thereof.

To take a break, stop in the village's cozy tea room; it serves restorative snacks, light meals, and beverages.

Before leaving Kensington, stop at the fairy-tale-sized Noyes Children's Library. Built in 1893, specifically as a children's library, it still serves only pre-schoolers. It features story-telling hours and ten thousand volumes for tots. At the other extreme is the massive Temple of the Church of Jesus Christ of Latter-Day Saints, in the Mormon faith, on a fifty-seven-acre site soaring above the Beltway. The temple is open to members only, but you can admire its marble-finish exterior, gold-plated steel spires, and handsomely landscaped grounds. *Maryland*

Antique Village, 3750-3776 Howard Ave., Old Kensington; (301) 949-5333.

Noyes Children's Library, Carroll and Montgomery avenues; (301) 929-5533. Open Tuesday, Thursday, and Saturday 9 a.m.-5 p.m.

Temple of the Church of Jesus Christ of the Latter-Day Saints, 9900 Stonybrook Dr.; (301) 587-0411. No nearby Metro Station, but call for Metrobus information: (202) 637-7000.

97 / America's Most Famous Private Home

Mount Vernon

More than a million people a year visit Mount Vernon, home of George Washington, to tour the handsome house and well-maintained grounds, which have been owned since 1858 by the Mount Vernon Ladies Association.

The house and surrounding acreage, sixteen miles from Washington, D.C., had been in the family for nearly ninety years by the time George Washington inherited them in 1761. He ran this eight-thousand-acre farm until the Revolution called him to duty; Washington retired here in 1797, two years before his death.

During his residency, hundreds of people made pilgrimages to Mount Vernon to meet their new leader. Washington and his wife, Martha, always rolled out the welcome mat. Visitors were invited to dinner in the banqueting hall, with its long wooden table and vivid green walls.

Today self-guided tours begin in this room and go outdoors to admire the view from the veranda Washington designed in 1777. Visitors then see the central hall, with the Bastille key on the wall (a gift from the Marquis de Lafayette) and the tiny parlor, then the downstairs bedroom and family dining room. Going upstairs, tour-goers view the austere bedroom in which Washington died in 1799. Back downstairs, they see Washington's study.

After you leave the house, you can explore the outbuildings, among them the kitchen, smokehouse, and slave quarters. You can also see the Washington tombs. The little museum includes an archaeological exhibit showing interesting stoneware, bottles, and pipes salvaged near the slave quarters.

Mount Vernon draws huge crowds, so avoid weekends and get there when it opens. *Virginia*

Mount Vernon, sixteen miles south of downtown D.C. along George Washington Memorial Parkway; (703) 780-2000 for hours and information. Adults $7; children, $3. No nearby Metro Station. On Gray Line daily tour route; (202) 289-1995.

98 / Go Back to Old Virginia

Old Town Alexandria

Old Town Alexandria seems like a set for a colonial American operetta. You expect characters in eighteenth-century waistcoats and tricornes to stride out of the quaint houses singing rousing patriotic arias. Your dream is shattered when a tour bus pulls in to remind you that Alexandria is a dynamic entertainment and historic center—and that any people in costume are tour guides taking groups on Doorways of Virginia tours.

To book a Doorways tour, stop at the Ramsay House Visitor's Center (221 King St. 9 a.m.-9 p.m.); or pick up an easy-to-follow walking-tour map for a self-guided tour.

Next door is the Carlyle House, the Georgian-Palladian mansion where General Edward Braddock and five governors strategized the French and Indian War campaigns. Tours are offered every half-hour; Tuesday-Saturday 10 a.m.-5 p.m.

Key sights include Christ Church, where George Washington worshipped and Robert E. Lee was confirmed. Lee's boyhood home (607 Oronoco St.) is a museum crammed with rare antiques (tours Monday-Saturday 10 a.m.-4 p.m., Sunday 1-4 p.m.).

Gadsby's Tavern Museum (134 North St.), where George Washington was fêted in February 1799, shortly before his death, is a restaurant offering colonial dishes.

When clipper ships put in here, Alexandria was the third busiest port in colonial America. Today, the waterfront bustles with fresh excitement. In a restored 1918 U.S. Navy factory for torpedo shells, 150 artists now work and sell their paintings, pottery, and other wares.

Before leaving, tour the 330-foot-high George Washington Masonic Memorial; the view's great.

Virginia

Old Town Alexandria, Metro Station: King Street. By car: Take George Washington Memorial Parkway or Jefferson Davis Highway south. Biking and hiking trails from D.C.; on Gray Line tour route.

99 / America's Most Renowned Burial Ground

Arlington National Cemetery

Especially evocative at Arlington National Cemetery are the rows of simple headstones marking the graves of 250,000 soldiers, from the Revolutionary War to the Persian Gulf War.

Crowded Tourmobiles roaming the grounds can make the cemetery seem out of sync with its solemn purpose. For a quieter visit, arrive early and walk to sites in this 612-acre burial ground. (Pick up a map at the Visitor's Center.)

Mesmerizing rituals at The Tomb of the Unknowns. In a tomb carved from a white marble block are the remains of a serviceman from World War I, World War II, and the Korean and Vietnam wars. Twenty-four hours a day, a soldier of the Old Guard protects the tomb. The sentinel marches twenty-one steps and faces the tomb for twenty-one seconds to symbolize a twenty-one gun salute, the nation's highest military honor. Every hour (every half-hour in summer) the guard changes in an intricate ceremony.

Memorials nearby honor the Challenger astronauts and the servicemen killed trying to free the American hostages in Iran.

Arlington House (Robert E. Lee Memorial) tops the hill. This Greek Revival home was built between 1802 and 1817 by George Washington Parke Custis, the adopted son of George Washington. His daughter, Mary, and her husband, Robert E. Lee, lived here with their children.

Pierre Charles L'Enfant's tomb was placed in front of the mansion to overlook the capital he designed.

John F. Kennedy's austere tomb with its eternal flame attracts crowds. This robs its serenity. Nearby are the graves of Jacqueline Kennedy Onassis and Robert F. Kennedy. *Virginia*

Arlington National Cemetery, (703) 692-0931. Grounds open daily, 8 a.m.-5 p.m. January-March; 8 a.m.-7 p.m. April-September. Free.

Arlington House, 9:30 a.m.-4:30 p.m. October-March; 9:30 a.m.-6 p.m. April-September. Metro Station: Arlington Cemetery.

100 / More Behind-the-Scenes Touring

Lesser-Known Government Buildings

Most visitors to D.C. think they've done it all if they explore three government buildings–the Capitol, the Supreme Court, and the White House. But here are a few experiences to be found at lesser-known government facilities.

Department of Defense—The Pentagon Lace up your sneakers! This seventy-five-minute tour takes you through one and a half miles of corridors and rooms. You might get a glimpse at one of the buildings 7,754 windows, or drink at one of the 690 drinking fountains. Guides (active-duty servicemen or servicewomen) keep you in sight so you do not try to wander off to play "war games."

Highlights on the tour include scale models of planes and warships, and the Hall of Heroes for Medal of Honor recipients. Off I-395, Arlington, Va.; (703) 694-1776. Free. Photo I.D. required for adults. Metro Station: Pentagon.

U.S. Department of the Interior Tours of the building's architecture and its hallway murals (showing 1930s-style epic cattle drives, gold panning, and dam building) require two weeks notice. The museum's collection traces the history of the multi-faceted Interior Department, which includes the National Park Service, Bureau of Indian Affairs, and the U. S. Geological Survey. Entrance at 18th and C streets NW; (202) 208-4743. Free. Metro Station: Farragut West or Foggy Bottom.

National Museum of Health and Medicine This is a fascinating "must" for those interested in American military history as far back as the War of 1812. Exhibits include (be forewarned) limbs severed in battle and an array of frightening old medical instruments. The Museum is located in Building 54, Walter Reed Army Medical Center; entrance at 6825 16th St. NW (Building 54 is on Dahlia St.); (202) 576-2348. Open 10 a.m.-5:30 p.m. daily; closed December 25. Metro Station: Takoma Park; free transfer to museum's bus.

101 / More Wild Times

Theodore Roosevelt Island and Potomac Parks

Theodore Roosevelt Island This wilderness preserve was authorized by Congress in 1932 as a memorial to President Theodore Roosevelt's dedication to conservation. TR's administration created the U.S. Forest Service, five national parks, fifty-one bird refuges, and four game preserves. Pack a picnic and a fishing pole. (Those sixteen and older need a permit.)

Birdwatchers: Take binoculars. The park has miles of quiet hiking trails amid marshlands, swamps, and forest. This is also a habitat for many small animals such as squirrels, rabbits, foxes, and muskrats.

In the Statuary Garden is Roosevelt's seventeen-foot bronze statue set off by tablets inscribed with his philosophies on nature, manhood, youth, and state.

Theodore Roosevelt Island, accessible only from northbound lane of George Washington Memorial Parkway; footbridge goes from parking lot to island; (703) 285-2598. Open 8 a.m.-dusk.

Maryland

West and East Potomac Parks Right in D.C. in the shadow of the Jefferson Memorial are 720 acres bisected by the Tidal Basin. There are thirteen hundred cherry trees in West Potomac Park (site of many of the week-long Cherry Blossom Festival events) and eighteen hundred in East Potomac Park. The cherry blossoms are an appetizer to a host of year-round activities: tennis, golf, jogging, hiking, biking, and more.

Peaceful West Potomac Park, dotted with Nobel Prize monuments, will house the grand new FDR Memorial. Haines Point, at the southern tip, is a peaceful, restorative outpost and the site of Seward Johnson's *The Awakening,* a sculptured figure emerging from the ground.

West and East Potomac Parks are south of Independence Avenue, between the Potomac River and Tidal Basin; information (202) 426-6841; tennis and golf, (202) 544-5962. Metro Station: Smithsonian.

Index